Southern Interiors

TORI MELLOTT *with* MARIO LÓPEZ-CORDERO

Southern Interiors

A Celebration of Personal Style

SCHUMACHER

CONTENTS

"In a good Southern interior, you will always find a bit of the ancient regime bumping up against the next generation."

W hen my pal Tori Mellott asked me to write the foreword for a book about Southern creatives at home, I was, of course, exceedingly flattered. I've known Tori for almost 20 years—we first met while working together at *Domino* magazine—and was excited to see the place I grew up in come alive through her lens. But then, I got worried. Distilling the ethos behind vernacular isn't easy, but it's especially complicated when it comes to the South. Flipping through the layouts, though, I was delighted to see a variety of design styles that don't necessarily swing toward the Southern cliché of garden clubbers sipping sweet tea from crystal highballs while lamenting the passage of bygone days, but rather harness a collective vibe of modernity.

The truth about Southern style—and the way it looks forward and backward simultaneously— is a sticky wicket to pin down. I know this because it's a wicket I myself tried to pin down in a recent job, which involved the renovation of a 10-room boutique hotel called the Celestine, located deep in the heart of New Orleans's French Quarter. Closely following the rituals of Louisiana style and hospitality, this hotel's quorum of owners had hired me to design rooms that would look "traditional but not dusty, like how New Orleans feels, welcoming and a little kooky." That directive, I realized, could just as well be the mission statement for an entire regional design ideology. But what does that *actually* look like? Well, I can tell you, the usual tropes—rocking chairs on the porch, vases filled with magnolia branches—are low-hanging fruit. *Real* Southern style, just like the interiors in this book, is far more nuanced.

Which brings me to my next point: Tropey or not, storytelling is another truism of the South, and antiques (whether inherited or picked up) are one way to impart that famously gothic narrative. They come with history. They invite you to wonder, to imagine what was going on before you were there, both the excellent *and* (especially when discussing the South) the atrocious. Thusly, in a good Southern interior, you will always find a bit of the ancient regime bumping up against the next generation. The best versions aren't suspended in amber, though: Great-Grandmother's formal Chippendale chairs are passed down, repurposed, and relaxed, modernized with linen slipcovers or a coat of paint.

One afternoon, after installing the last few rooms of the Celestine, I stepped out onto the balcony to marvel at a thunderstorm dumping lashings of rain onto the courtyard below. To my surprise, a group of white-haired guests spilled out into the pouring rain from Peychaud's, the bar attached to the hotel. There in the courtyard, surrounded by soaked fan palms, the group started twirling, dancing, and screaming with laughter. It was an image I won't soon forget, calling to mind that other Southern truth: If you are raised with the rules of civilized society, you will also have the confidence to break them. To me, the thoughtfully arranged homes on the following pages seem to reflect just that—a region filled with people who, while cognizant of the past, are determined to rewrite the definition of the present.

Sara Ruffin Costello
New Orleans, March 2024

INTRODUCTION: TORI MELLOTT

First, let's get one thing straight: Despite being the author of a book on Southern style, I am Southern only if southwestern Pennsylvania counts. I was born and raised in Aliquippa, a hamlet near Pittsburgh, and while I counted Julia Sugarbaker, Daisy Duke, and the entire 1980 Dallas Cowboys cheerleading squad among the women I admired in my childhood, the only thing this Pittsburgh gal has in common with residents of the American South is an occasionally funny vernacular. (Yinz guys know what I mean?) But as a design editor who has spent the last 25 years traipsing through hundreds of houses decorated by the very best designers in the world, I have to tell you, it's always been the Southern ones that really set my heart on fire. They capture an ineffable quality that's hard to define but is impossible to ignore.

I had my first brush with the South at six years old when I visited the Atlanta home of my second cousin once removed, Melba Jean Brooks—arguably the most beautiful woman in our family—who had fled Pittsburgh decades earlier at age 18 to marry a Georgia man. One summer, my parents took me and my siblings on a trip down the Eastern Seaboard, visiting relatives here and there until we arrived at Melba Jean's house in Atlanta, our final destination. It was the fanciest house I had ever laid eyes on. I didn't know homes could be so vast, smell so good, or be so filled with light. I remember sitting on a large sofa that was covered in a quilted floral chintz. The glaze on the fabric felt cool and crisp on the backs of my legs. Melba Jean's living room had John Fowler–yellow walls, a fine wool Chinese Peking rug, and a pair of ginger jar lamps with pleated ivory silk shades—the stuff that Reagan-era dreams are made of. Melba Jean seemed to float from the kitchen to the living room as she served us iced tea on a gleaming tray. I remember her megawatt smile and the way everything felt so carefree and effortless in her home. I felt and saw there an intangible quality inherent to the South—a kind of easy sophistication that seemed natural and the opposite of intimidating—and though I couldn't articulate it at the time, I knew I wanted it.

Fast-forward to 1998, the year I moved to New York City, when I met one of my closest friends, Elizabeth Blitzer. Biddy (Southerners love a good nickname) is a Baton Rouge native who could charm the pants off a brick wall. Not only does she make everyone feel special, but she also makes throwing a party for 75 of your closest friends look easy. Pro tips: Make sure your guests don't know you're stressed and always have delicious food on hand (even if that means ordering in a bunch of Popeyes fried chicken and serving it on a silver platter). Biddy showed me what Southern charm, grace, hospitality, and effortless living really were. I'm still a novice, but suffice it to say, the way Southerners live is my lodestar. There's a grace and an ease about everything they do, from the way they say a simple "hello" to the way they serve pimento-cheese sandwiches to strangers.

Southerners have a similarly insouciant approach to matters of taste. I was a baby editor when I first encountered the work of the late Albert Hadley—a New Yorker by way of Nashville and the patron saint of American style—on the cover of the February/March 2000 issue of *Elle Decor*. The photo was unforgettable: a giant swathe of robin's-egg blue on the wall, surrounded by black-and-white artwork paired with a sleek console and X-base sling stool that looked as though it had been dipped in white paint. It was a revelation. Like almost everyone who runs in design circles, I became an Albert Hadley disciple almost overnight. And don't get me started on the time I met the late, great journalist and renowned tastemaker Julia Reed. She was like a William Faulkner character come to life: a voice so raspy, a tongue so fierce, and a wit so sharp I was half in awe of her and half shaking in my shoes. She carried herself like one of her rooms—a cool mix of patrician and bohemian with plenty of room left over for a healthy dollop of humor. What these legendary Southerners had in common was an aesthetic rooted in the personal, committed to individual experience in a way that was respectful of the tenets of design, but at the same time, they had no problem throwing those tenets out the window.

What we are talking about is *character*—and character was my number one requirement when I began seeking out interiors to include in this book. Each and every home featured in this book is so deeply personal, beautiful, and unique—there isn't a single one that feels expected—and that's just the way I like it. I truly hope that reading the stories of the houses and the people who have created them brings you as much joy as it has for me. And if it doesn't, well then, as my Southern friends would say with a wry smile, bless your heart.

From early on in my career, I was captivated by the soulful design ethos of these late Southern tastemakers.
CLOCKWISE FROM TOP LEFT: Julia Reed enlisted an all-star team of Southern talent—architect James F. Carter and
designers Courtney Coleman and Bill Brockschmidt—to help dream up her "Delta Folly" on the Mississippi.
Gerrie Bremermann's groundbreaking penchant for layering modern art with European antiques and understated neutrals
was on full display in a client's living room. The sitting room of Tennessee-born Albert Hadley's apartment on the
Upper East Side remains an icon of design. Leave it to antiquarian Furlow Gatewood to transform a dirt-floored greenhouse
on his family's 11-acre property in southwest Georgia into the impossibly refined "Peacock House."

"Heat and rural isolation tend to brew up the best of the best. Certainly, eccentricity and patina are part of the diet here."

—Bobby McAlpine

Kerry P. Moody

Antiques Dealer, Decorator, and Stylist

"**M**y family has been in Louisiana since the end of the 18th century; I am descended from enslaved people and French settlers. I live in an early 19th-century Creole cottage in Bywater, a classic foursquare plan of rooms with the fireplaces located in the center of house instead of the outside walls. There are 'cabinets' (or small rooms) at the back joined by an enclosed gallery that now serves as my kitchen. The walls are bargeboards allegedly salvaged from the Mississippi River, which was a common early building technique in this part of New Orleans. The walls would have then been covered with painted canvas or plaster to keep out the wind. (Mine are plaster.) I'm a confirmed bachelor, but wouldn't say I live alone, as the house is alive with friends, family, and *things*!"

Moody found the 18th-century Creole portrait in France. "Some people think it could be an ancestor, and maybe it could—in fact, he has become one," says Moody. The 19th-century iron-and-leather ceremonial wedding necklace from Ghana, a gift from a friend, "sometimes whispers to me."

Tell us your favorite things about living in the South.
Does New Orleans really qualify as a typical Southern milieu? It has always been polyglot in every sense of the word: culturally, historically, and racially. That being said, the easy answer about what I love about being in New Orleans (or our version of the South) is the architecture, music, cuisine, and the crazy wonderful, eccentric people.

What defines Southern living for you?
For one thing, style really does matter. Developing your sense of style and sharing it with friends means never asking if it's too much trouble to pull out the right glass for champagne or a saucer for the coffee cup, even if the cup is chipped. The silver may need polishing, but it's on the table!

What should every Southern house have and why?
The essentials of every household, even if it's a pup tent, are nice silver flatware, a few good glasses, big white linen napkins, a monumental soup ladle, and of course good conversation.

How has the South shaped your aesthetic?
People here have absorbed the ethos that it's not a matter of finance but romance that is to be primarily appreciated. Cash is great, but creativity is better. The other marvelous thing about New Orleans is our devotion to dramatic effect and illusion. There is something about living in an old city that was once the queen of the South that continues to taunt us with temptations to grandeur. A small cottage like mine can transport someone to another realm, and even if they would never want to duplicate it, they still can enjoy it.

Tell us about a few things in your house that make you beam with pride.
Like most people who love their houses, everything has a story, and a connection with my life. I love the Creole painting above my mantel; some people think it could be an ancestor, and maybe it could—in fact, he has essentially become one. I first saw it in France in the collection of some acquaintances and didn't bite. It haunted me, and the next year I went back and bought it. The copper in my kitchen I've collected piece by piece, and it holds stories of gumbos and bouillabaisses and good times around my table. I'm also moved by the ceremonial iron-and-leather necklace from Ghana that was a gift. It sometimes whispers to me.

What's a Southern rule you love to break?
The one tradition I occasionally transgress, but with great difficulty since I am naturally loquacious, is the long goodbye. By the end of the evening, as delightful as it has been, a simple *à bientôt* is sometimes enough.

Off the top of your head, give us five words that sum up the South.
Only five words! Even Genesis starts out with 10. But here goes: pride, pleasure-loving, prejudice, poetry, and playfulness.

In the back parlor stair hall, a jib door conceals a coat closet. Moody bought the Directoire *lit de repos* while on his first buying trip to France.

Your Sugar Ration
is 2 lbs. per month

The back parlor leads to the kitchen gallery, with an early 19th-century Louisiana *garde manger* that Moody found on the street and restored. The oil painting is a copy of an original by Impressionist artist Frédéric Bazille. OPPOSITE: "Cabinets" like this small room at the back of the kitchen are typical of Creole houses.

In the library, dining room, and sitting room, antique French crystal and silver mingle with 19th-century pottery, a brass hunting horn, and a collection of African arrows. OPPOSITE: Moody declined to electrify the Empire-style tole chandelier, preferring instead to dine by candlelight.

Betsy Brown
Interior Designer

"My house began life as a 1940s, post–World War II brick structure with a low-pitched roof that I bought for its beautiful view of the city. I raised the exterior brick to create parapet walls, added a slate roof, and put three French doors across the front. I love classicism, so it worked. As to the interiors, I like intelligent, soulful spaces that don't require a staff to maintain. Peace, comfort, time-worn furniture, and beautiful objects are what motivate me the most."

In the living room, a painting by Jean-Marc Louis and a drawing Brown found at a flea market in Paris soften the modernist angles of the mantel, while an English Regency chair covered in supple black leather bridges the difference.

Brown outfitted the anteroom to the primary bedroom as a library, anchored by a Rose Uniacke pendant and an antique French drop-leaf table. Custom slipper chairs in a breezy ticking stripe lighten the muted color scheme.

How has the South shaped your point of view?
I started my career in the 1980s, when the women in my neighborhood didn't work outside the home. I chafe against expectations to do things the way they "should" be done. I prefer to break the rules or, to be honest, invent new ones. I didn't look to my neighbors' houses for inspiration, but to those designed by greats like Billy Baldwin, Angelo Donghia, Anthony Hail, John Dickinson, and Albert Hadley.

Southern hospitality is a cliché, but also legendary for a reason. Why do you think that is?
The practice of Southern hospitality is a beautiful one that, like many aspects of our culture, has a painful past. It began at a time when many white Southern families didn't pay their workers, which freed them to indulge in the most elaborate kind of entertaining. Society has changed; traditions have adjusted. Southerners now entertain on a less ostentatious scale while still maintaining the passion they've always had. Cooking has become richer, too, incorporating processes and foods from other cultures and fully recognizing their origins—like the okra, beans, greens, and cornmeal that people of color introduced. Diversity and acceptance have added depth to the practice of Southern hospitality, but there's still work to be done.

Imagination game: You're plopped into the living room of some stranger's house and allowed to roam at will. How do you know it's Southern?
If there are portraits and gardening books, it's a Southern house! Is that portrait life-size? Then it's *definitely* a Southerner's house! Full disclosure: I have wonderful framed drawings of my daughters and a gazillion garden books that were my mother's in my house.

Can you tell us about a Southern tradition passed down to you—familial or otherwise—that you adopted, and why?
Collecting! My mother was an antiques dealer who was obsessed with Billy Baldwin's rooms. At one point, my sisters and I thought she must be having an affair with the man! From her, I inherited an appreciation for design and a desire to collect. She collected shells, birds' nests, plants, and furniture. Every road trip we took was punctuated by stops at small, dusty antique shops. When I was young, it was actually quite painful to follow her around, staring at things I didn't understand or want, but somehow it took root in me. Southerners value unique objects that elevate everyday life.

What role do you think character plays in Southern houses?
Nothing makes me more comfortable in a home than authenticity. Forget perfection—it doesn't even matter if it's well designed! Books stacked on every surface, strange collections grouped on tabletops, a puzzle or a game of chess in progress, yard flowers in a vase—it's the evidence of real life that gives a room soul. I once had an older client, Helen, who took me under her wing when I was a young designer. She'd grown up in New Orleans where collecting is a fierce pastime. At her instruction, I had a giant, upholstered plywood shield constructed—padded with flannel and covered in green wool—to display her husband's vast antique pipe collection. We hung it over a beautiful green strié sofa with a long bullion fringe around the base. It was magnificent. She also hung her collection of sterling silver tea strainers on her Christmas tree every year. She didn't follow rules and encouraged me not to, either. The lesson? If a space is a genuine expression of the owner, everyone will be comfortable there.

The bright and airy sunroom, with a mid-century kilim, rattan armchair, and an antique draper's table, is a balm for Brown's mild claustrophobia and affords stunning views.

The sitting room converts easily to a guest room, thanks to a long custom daybed composed of two twin mattresses. A slate top on the Saarinen tulip table artfully defies expectations; the photograph is by Stuart Redler. OPPOSITE: In the mostly monochrome living room, a 19th-century brass Dutch repoussé mirror is a foil for a Serge Mouille floor lamp and sleek upholstery.

A custom coverlet and diaphanous curtains envelop the primary bedroom in a tactile softness.
OPPOSITE: Brown blends eras and influences in the guest bedroom: a modern
four-poster hung with a gauzy canopy, complete with handmade tassels, a George III cabinet,
and a Louis XV–style armchair covered in an ikat from Uzbekistan.

Beatrix Ost

Artist and Designer

" **I** am originally from Munich, Germany. I moved to the United States in 1975. My husband and I bought an apartment in New York City, but we quickly realized Manhattan is too dense. So, in 1979, we bought a famous house on the Hudson River in Cold Springs. However, the house burned to the ground; afterward, I took a pendulum and dangled it over a map of America on the kitchen table and that's how we found our way to Virginia. It was pure adventure! Our house dates from 1815 and was built by James Dinsmore, one of Thomas Jefferson's master craftsmen, who designed buildings for the University of Virginia and Poplar Forest, the Jefferson plantation in Bedford County. This house has gravitas, it holds you by the roots."

Ost walks her dogs down the driveway of the house, which was built in 1815. It retains original millwork by James Dinsmore, a carpenter also employed by Thomas Jefferson at Monticello and Poplar Forest, the Jefferson summer retreat.

A custom table by
Michele Oka Doner
anchors the Great Hall,
where doors are flung
open to the outdoors and
Ost's preferred method
of climate control—
a ceiling fan—circulates
the fragrant air.

Tell us your favorite things about living in the South.
Charlottesville is an intelligent town. It is Jefferson's town, a university town, and a writer's town. It's very historic and very beautiful. There is so much nature and so much beauty everywhere. If I need flowers, I just go to the garden and pick them. I love early spring; friends from New York come down and we always have Easter parties. And fall—we have fall forever. It lasts until Christmas practically. Charlottesville is also very centrally located—it doesn't feel remote. I have German friends who bought a farm in Georgia, but they were so far out on their gorgeous land, they had to have a little airplane just to get to the grocery store! Distances in America can be so vast.

How do your surroundings enhance your sense of creativity?
I'm very much inspired by the landscape. My last two exhibitions are called "I Could Have Been a Tree Instead," which means to imply that we are like trees, but trees are our superiors and we can learn from them. A tree needs a healthy environment. It is an example from nature that, in many ways, is living a human life. Or perhaps the other way around.

What's special about your house?
It's a historic house that was exquisitely well-built and is exquisitely well-preserved. I think it's gorgeous the way it sits in the countryside, and how it slants on an east-west axis. It has a grand center hall, and the windows go all the way down and all the way up so you can regulate the flow of air. From the main hall there are two staircases that rise to the next floor and the center of the house, to what was the summer room, where centuries ago former residents would have sat with mint juleps, fanning themselves.

How and why do you entertain?
I love having wonderful parties with wonderful food. I have sit-down dinners and I like a long table, so you can talk to the person across from you as well as your neighbor. The most important thing is that people feel at home and not stifled. For instance, we would never say, "please don't sit there." Everything is here to be used for comfort and enjoyment—my house is your house.

Tell us what a Southern house should have and why.
I think every Southern house should have ceiling fans, not air conditioners—and in every large room, there should be two ceiling fans. And you have to have books and something to recline on while you look out into the countryside. We have a breakfast room where you can see the sun come up over the Blue Ridge Mountains. It's magnificent.

Ost's art—including wax busts and large-scale paintings—populate the Great Hall, where she also displays a whimsical and century-spanning collection of children's chairs.

In the library, a mural by John Owen surrounds the fireplace and mantel,
while a set of Josef Hoffmann chairs and table beckon from the corner.
OPPOSITE: Owen painted another mural in a guest bedroom library; Ost artfully
set it off with gleaming tea paper on the walls below the dado.

After a violent storm blew down a tree on the property, Ost had a tree house—
and beguiling garden folly—built around the remaining stump. OPPOSITE: A gate
made of sculptural branches leads the way to the swimming pool.

Stan Dixon

Architect

"I'm Southern, born and raised in Tennessee, and have always been in the South. I live with my wife, Shannon, and our dog, Winston, in a house built in 1928 with a French Normandy flair. We lived here for 13 years with our two children before moving out for a yearlong renovation and addition. The current kitchen and breakfast room are half new construction and half renovation. All of the plaster was removed to insulate, rewire, and replumb the house, and the original wavy glass windows were refurbished throughout. It's designed for the easy entertaining of friends and family, with two fireplaces to enjoy in the cooler months and a garden in the warmer months. There are ample seating and conversation groupings throughout the house, and our large dining room, central to the floor plan, can seat as many as 16 people."

In his living room, an antique French mantel that Dixon purchased on a trip to
France with his wife, Shannon, bridges the divide between a sculptural gilt Rococo-style mirror
and a sharp-angled cocktail table by Ludwig Mies van der Rohe.

Tell us a few of your favorite things about living in the South.
The changing landscape and climate in all four seasons, the verdant city I live in, the culture of hospitality, and the genuine warmth of Southern people.

How has the South shaped your point of view?
I have always appreciated the South's love of timeless architecture and design, which I incorporate into my own work. Living in a region that embraces so many influences has exposed me to different styles and allowed me to build a visual library that I can now draw on in my practice.

What do you love most about your house?
The antique French marble mantel in our living room is a piece my wife and I found together; we appreciate its formality but also love its simplicity. We also love our kitchen—when we renovated it, we wanted it to be exceptionally beautiful while retaining its functionality. I enjoy using it every day.

What should every Southern house have?
A porch, a gracious entryway, a fireplace, and a walk-in pantry.

Tell us about a tradition that you adopted and why.
An important value from my childhood that I carry forward is celebrating moments, small and large, with my family and friends. We're not overly formal, but we enjoy entertaining and creating a comfortable, inviting atmosphere that makes any gathering memorable.

What's a Southern rule you love to break?
I don't subscribe to the requirement of handwritten invitations, and I don't think all the crystal has to match.

What's the quirkiest thing about your house?
Unlike many modern houses, where the inhabitants tend to park and enter through the garage, we don't use our garage and instead prefer to enter and exit through the front door.

If you had to leave the South, what would you miss the most?
Definitely the Southern cooking: iced tea and fried chicken! Secondly, the casual congeniality and understated sophistication.

What do outsiders get wrong about the South?
Just because we're talkin' slow, doesn't mean we're thinkin' slow! And, more generally, the idea that we lack worldliness.

Give us a few words that sum up the region and your home.
The South: beautiful, kind, and diverse. Our house: happy, gracious, light, warm, and welcoming.

Chairs and a table Dixon scored at Atlanta's famed Scott Antique Markets—known locally as "Scott's"—create a workspace in the living room. Dixon and his wife, Shannon, painted the abstract work on the left; the other pieces include an antique French oil and a painting by Carolyn Carr.

In the dining room,
a French screen painted
with a maritime scene
that Dixon bought for
his wife as a gift during
the house's renovation
takes center stage.
The "window" on the left
is really a swing door
fitted with mirrors that
leads to the pantry
and was added to create
a sense of symmetry.

The breakfast room off the kitchen is central to the flow of the house.
OPPOSITE: To soften the geometry of sleek modern cabinetry, Dixon installed custom
oak trestle table legs under the island counter, helping to reduce
the island's large scale and visually connecting the space with adjacent rooms.

The bay window in the primary bedroom perfectly accommodates an antique French sofa, which provides extra seating during the day, but doesn't impede pulling the curtains closed at night for privacy. OPPOSITE: In a daughter's room, a sconce installed on top of the silk bed canopy is a splashy flourish that also offers function.

Beth Webb

Interior Designer

"**M**y husband, Chuck Hanavich, and I live in a glass house that he built before we got married. It was designed by architect James Choate to commune with the wild landscape as a series of modernist wood, stone, and glass pavilions. We're in the wild, verdant Lowcountry, between a rice pond and a marsh. Full-height windows offer views of live oaks from ground to sky; they're spectacular vantage points for watching the deer, alligators, birds, and changing seasons."

Texture abounds in the study, with walls paneled in cedar, a fireplace lined with North Carolina granite, and a natural fiber rug underfoot. Ample armchairs on either side of the walnut and wenge desk ensure a cushy perch for working.

The house's steel and glass facade offers ample views of the
Lowcountry terrain that surrounds it. OPPOSITE: In the foyer, a cowhide rug
softens honed concrete floors without sacrificing rusticity.

In the aptly named great room, another granite fireplace highlights truly soaring ceilings. No fewer than three sofas help divide the vast space into more intimate seating arrangements that bring proportions down to earth.

What defines Southern living for you and how does that play out in your house?

I draw deeply on sense of place. My aesthetic is rooted in monochromatic palettes and sensual textures attuned to the environment—cypress and Spanish-moss-draped live oaks, marsh grasses, and water. When I moved into our house, we replaced Sheetrock finishes with cedar and wenge and white oak to create a warm, intimate environment with the texture and patina of wood that reflects the setting, while ivory and cream fabrics create a serene frame for the views.

What do you love most about where you live?

The seamless relationship between landscape, decorating, living, cooking, and entertaining is what I've always loved about the South. The connection to the land sets the tone for so much of the lifestyle—the warmth, the heavy scent of magnolia and honeysuckle on a soft summer night, or the scent of the earth, like a comforting blanket of vegetation and soil. The food culture is an obvious extension of this—a perfect summer tomato sandwich, blueberries fresh from the garden, fried okra. To this day, recipes passed down through generations for family and friends and gathering around an exquisitely set table are defining traditions for me.

How did growing up in the South shape your point of view?

I was raised in Lookout Mountain, Tennessee, population—back then—1,600. When I was a kid, there was no such thing as a stranger, no one locked their doors, and we walked or rode our bikes everywhere. We were like free-range chickens, spending endless hours building forts in the woods and midsummer nights chasing fireflies. I suppose our parents had a general idea of where we might be at any given time, but as long as we were home for dinner,

all was right with the world. My fondest memories are of waking up at my maternal grandparents' house, snug in a bed dressed in freshly ironed sheets, the warmth of the sun coming up and streaming through the windows, the grandfather clock ticking just outside the bedroom door. That sense of peace and sanctuary is still at the core of everything I design.

Describe your approach to entertaining.

In the South growing up, "entertaining" always meant *at home*. Core experiences for me were Sunday suppers at my grandparents', my mother's Christmas lunch for fifty, and Thanksgivings at the family farm in Alabama. Today, our homes are the heart of our extended family—backdrops for guests and dogs and lots of dinners. Whether that means setting a table with antique china and polished silver or always keeping the bar well-stocked, it's all about connection and conversation.

Share five things that bring you happiness at home.

Setting an exquisite table. Welcoming guests to clink glasses in front of the fire. Brunch al fresco on the lawn amid the sound of cicadas and birdsong. Our family of 17 gathered around a refectory table at Christmas. My dog, Biscuit, at my feet while I work.

What are a few things every Southern house should have?

A bar cart for the obvious reasons! We are prodigious drinkers. Monogrammed linens—we do not use paper napkins at our house *ever*. Your grandmother's silver. I grew up using the sterling flatware on a daily basis. Dogs. I've always had dogs and always will! And antiques—furniture imbued with a sense of history and soul—are an intrinsic part of a house's narrative.

An early 19th-century demilune table feels right at home amid the minimalist
environs of the study—and makes for a genteel bar cart. OPPOSITE: Curtains crafted
from a circus-tent's-worth of linen soften angular windows.

In the dining room, Christian Liaigre campaign chairs amplify
the campsite feel. OPPOSITE: The kitchen cabinetry and appliances are
completely cloaked in wenge for a seamless, sensual effect.

A guest bedroom flush with suede, cedar, rattan, wicker, and Kuba cloth embodies Webb's philosophy of enriching a panoply of neutrals with lush, cosseting texture. The art is by Jane Ingols.

Chelsea Handegan

Interior Designer

"I live in an 1854 Italianate row home designed by Edward C. Jones with my husband, Jack, my daughter, Hattie, and our dog and cat. I was born and raised in the Lowcountry, and aside from an embarrassingly short stint at a small liberal arts college near Boston, I've never left."

A mixture of refined and down-to-earth elements makes the most of the historic living room, whose original crown moldings and mantel date to 1854.

In true Charleston style, the Italianate row house opens onto a porch or "piazza" as locals call it—which allows for extra ventilation in the subtropical climate.

What do you love most about where you live?
The dialect has a softness not found elsewhere. At freshman orientation in college, I laughed aloud when I heard someone's genuine use of "wicked," a word I had never heard outside the context of Halloween. Similarly, tourists and transplants are easily identifiable by their pronunciation of "Charleston." Natives roll right through the "r," while foreigners pause for a pirate-like "arr." The kindness of strangers is also so different here: I vividly recall waiting to hold the door to my Massachusetts dorm open for a student several steps behind me, who looked at me like I had two heads. Southerners never hesitate to hold the door open for others, greet passersby on the sidewalk, or sign up for the meal train of a neighbor they barely know.

What defines Southern living for you?
Homes are meant to be lived in and used, and if that means there is some imperfection or wonkiness, so be it. My home, with its steep stairs and just one full bathroom, could not be less practical for a family with a small child and an elderly dog. The powder room faucets (terrific unlacquered brass Victorian taps from England) started leaking two Thanksgivings ago, and we haven't turned the water back on to them since!

What's unique about your house?
Our house is 170 years old. With the help of one very profane Polish contractor, we painstakingly renovated it. People were madder than hell when I pulled up the 1950s black-and-white tile floors in the kitchen, powder room, and bathroom. My "I told you so" moment came when the excavation revealed the original heart pine floors underneath. The double parlor on the main floor possesses ornate plaster moldings and ceiling medallions. We had decades of built-up paint carefully scraped to better display the details of the plasterwork. The trade-off of the grand double parlor is that

I have a kitchen that is small even by New York City standards. We briefly entertained the idea of converting the dining room into a large eat-in kitchen à la many New York City brownstones, but I am immensely proud that we maintained the integrity of the floor plan. Toward the end of the renovation, I was fatigued by decision-making, so I painted the entry and stair hall a creamy white, but the sterility of it drove me crazy. I painted the walls apricot, and inspired by the painted floors of Furlow Gatewood, I had a decorative painter apply an oxblood faux marble design on the floors. It's a showstopper. Lastly, I am forced to say I love how I can feel the wind *inside* my house, as the Board of Architectural Review has no intention of allowing me to resolve such a *blessing*.

What's your entertaining ethos?
The entire process—from the planning to the cooking—should be fun, and no amount of pomp and circumstance can cover for a stressed-out hostess. I skip the hors d'oeurves and fine wines in favor of weenies and martinis, throw open the French doors, turn on some music, and call it a party.

Can you tell us about a family tradition you've adopted?
The engraved pewter porringer from my father's baptism, which was also used and engraved for my baptism and my daughter's baptism, is a prized possession and also a wonderful bowl for floating camellias. Nothing is too precious to be used.

What's a Southern rule you just flat out refuse to follow?
I have never in my life attended a football game.

Give us five words that sum up the South and your home there.
The South: welcoming, imperfect, historic, impractical, magical.
My house: welcoming, imperfect, historic, impractical, tall.

In the dining room, Handegan hung papier-mâché medallions of Hermes over Sabina Fay Braxton velvet panels, exalting painted newsprint to the level of marble and cleverly framing the mantel, above which hangs an early 19th-century English portrait.

Ticking stripes and toile make for a natural pairing in the guest room.
OPPOSITE: A collection of 18th-century Italian portraits adds a flourish to the stair hall,
with walls in subtle peach (Academy from Portola Paints).

In Hattie's room, Handegan embraced whimsy—like a stuffed swan soaring overhead—
and charm, furnished by vintage toys and Roman shades in a gingham check.
OPPOSITE: A wallpaper panel mounted on board is an artful backdrop for an antique
French daybed; the antique chandelier is Swedish.

A clean-lined canopy bed in the primary bedroom is hung with curtains trimmed in
graphic pompons for just a hint of a flourish that doesn't go over the top.
OPPOSITE: For the powder room, enveloped in a Penny Morrison wallpaper, Handegan
sourced English Victorian brass fittings; the antique giltwood mirror is French.

Chandra Johnson

Gallerist

"**M**y home is not just about aesthetics but also about thoughtful use of space. Each room is arranged to accommodate a range of activities: playdates, game nights, cocktail parties, or lounging on a Sunday afternoon. The South has taught me to really think about how I want to live and entertain in my home. So much credit goes to our designer, Barrie Benson, for skillfully merging traditional Southern design with modern elements. She and I are great collaborators and even opened a business together, Peg Norriss, a textile and wallcovering company that features designs by contemporary artists."

A chinoiserie-inspired mural wallpaper and puddling bed hangings in a rich velvet give the primary bedroom a glorious sense of romance that's held just in check with vintage furnishings that include an iconic Pedro Friedeberg hand chair.

Johnson, a gallerist, boasts a formidable art collection. In a hallway, the artworks (clockwise from top left) include pieces by Henri Matisse, Liz Nielsen, Franz Kline, Line Vautrin, Terry O'Neill, Malick Sidibé, Damian Stamer, and Brittany Little.

What do you love most about living in the South?
The people. There is a warmth and sophistication here that is magical. Southern hospitality—and Southern food—is a glorious experience. I also love how Southern cities strike a great balance between cosmopolitan flair and bucolic charm, making them ideal places for raising a family.

What does Southern living mean to you and how does that play out in your home?
For me, it revolves around a sense of comfort coupled with a love of environment and a genuine desire to share it with others. This philosophy strongly influenced the design of my home, which has been crafted to easily blend entertaining and everyday family living. From casual gatherings to formal affairs, our home is set up for diverse needs, providing functionality for any occasion. Our eclectic mix of cherished family heirlooms and a constantly growing art collection creates an atmosphere that feels like a true reflection of our lives, from past to present.

Tell us about a few things in your house that make you beam with pride.
I am very proud of the art collection that my husband, Jimmie, and I have built together over many years, which includes numerous Southern artists. Other highlights are heirloom treasures: my great-grandmother's silver, my grandmother's china, and a Steinway piano from Jimmie's grandmother.

How does where you live inform your creativity?
Opening the SOCO Gallery and bookshop in 2014 has given me the privilege of working with incredible artists and creatives from all over the world. The artists we exhibit experience a deep personal connection with the community, a phenomenon distinct to the South. This intimate interaction has been rewarding for both our artists and our audience and has stimulated a vibrant, creative environment.

Tell us what every Southern house should have and why.
Monogrammed linens for a personalized touch and fresh flowers to bring the outside in. Heirloom silver brings a sense of history and tradition, while pickle forks add a Southern touch to everyone's favorite side dish.

What's one of your most beloved family traditions?
The celebration of holidays with sit-down family dinners, Sunday suppers, and indulging in bacon for breakfast. A kitchen bustling with the preparations for a shared meal brings so much joy and creates a sense of togetherness.

What's a Southern rule you love to break?
I unapologetically put my silver and china in the dishwasher. To enjoy it daily, convenience won over the handwashing requisite.

What do outsiders get wrong about the South?
They underestimate the thriving cultural scene in the South. Despite assumptions about being culturally dormant, the South embraces contemporary art and creativity wholeheartedly. Opening SOCO Gallery challenged this stereotype—the space was received with open arms and an interested audience that shows the region's deep appreciation for artistic expression.

In the living room, a Louis XV–style mantel is backed in sleek antiqued mirror, encapsulating Barrie Benson's era-melding yin-yang approach. OPPOSITE: Benson augmented the mostly neutral palette with rosy shades of pink and glinting surfaces, like the brass-framed cocktail table.

A built-in bar bracketed by another painterly wallpaper makes for instant, easy entertaining. OPPOSITE: A vibrant orange wall sculpture by Donald Judd and ceiling painted by artist Damian Stamer are brilliant foils for staid antiques in the dining room.

In Jimmie Johnson's study, a vibrant red chair adds dash to a vintage desk and a rotating collection of contemporary photography. OPPOSITE: Fire-engine-red lacquered walls in the library flicker with candlelight when the Johnsons host dinner parties in the intimate—and charmingly surprising—venue.

Juxtaposing elements—
scalloped edges, a
simple canopy, a refresh-
ingly overscale print,
and contemporary art—
ensure that Johnson's
daughter's bedroom is
sweet and sophisticated.
OPPOSITE: Graphic
floral wallpaper and sharp
white stripes achieve
the same end in Johnson's
dressing room.

James F. Carter

Architect

"I live in Birmingham, which is large enough to qualify as a city but not so large as to have lost all of its small-town charm, in a house I designed that is primarily pre-Revolutionary American Georgian in style. In all my work, I think of the spaces I design as more of a backdrop for life rather than a piece of art that forces those living there to bend to it. I like tables and lamps where I need them and arrangements of furniture that encourage conversation. I like a room that accepts me in black tie or blue jeans. I don't mind mixing something very refined with something simple but personal if it suits my needs."

The exterior facade, a combination of whitewashed brick and painted wood, gives the impression that the house Carter designed, built in 2013, is centuries-old and evolved over time.

Black-and-white
stone floors make for
a grand foyer, but the
space's proportions
soften the effect and
make the whole
scene feel surprisingly
intimate and cozy.

What's one of your favorite things about living in the South?
My emotional connection to my past and its history here. I appreciate the respect people in the South have for a certain civility in their day-to-day behavior; my grandmother always said, "One should rise to the occasion—not sink to it." Despite what many think, the best Southern people usually accept others for who they are.

How are your Southern roots revealed in your work?
Anyone who's being creative must put something of themselves into the work or it will never seem honest and valid. Whenever I'm designing a dining room, for instance, I always think back to large holiday dinners at my grandparents with flowers, candles, and a table of 12. These memories help me determine the priorities of the space.

What's a Southern rule you love to break?
I'm a rule follower until someone thinks I am. Then I like to shake things up and go rogue.

What do you love most about your home?
People seem to think that my home is inviting, interesting, and somehow, an expression of me personally. I particularly enjoy living with things that belonged to both my parents and their respective families. Although my home is somewhat grand, everyone says that it "feels" rather cozy. It's the highest compliment.

Tell us five things every Southern house should have.
A gracious porch. One cozy room that encourages conversation. A certain lack of perfection. Open fires in the winter and a good breeze in the summer. And a host who knows how to make people feel welcome. All of these things make guests relax and enjoy themselves in your home, which should be the primary reason to entertain.

What's your approach to entertaining?
I don't really cook but I do know how to serve a cocktail. Although I have an occasional dinner party for 30 to 40, typically when friends are in town, I prefer to have eight in for drinks and then go out for dinner.

What's a common thread in many Southern houses?
Typically, there will be a lot of family photographs and college memorabilia that clue you in to the life history of the family. In my home, I have a wall of family photographs and numerous souvenirs from my travels over the last 30-something years. I have the grand and the great next to the simplest of sentimental things.

In the library, waxed antique oak paneling allows a collection of blue-chip antiques,
which Carter collected over the span of 25 years, to take center stage without becoming overbearing.
OPPOSITE: The room's overmantel was designed to frame an antique portrait.

Beadboard paneling and corner cupboards fitted with arched neo-Gothic panes in the kitchen have a layered, passed-down-through-the-centuries effect. OPPOSITE: Bare floors and built-in bookshelves tone down the dining room, which was scaled to embrace a painted Italian screen that Carter acquired on his travels.

Quirky coffered ceilings cap Carter's bathroom and dressing room; the built-in cupboards are covered in a Schumacher ticking stripe. OPPOSITE: A deep window recess accommodates an antique desk and armchair—and affords a splendid view.

The primary bedroom, with its sloping ceilings cloaked in an evocative shade
of green, cozy canopy bed, and charmingly off-kilter proportions,
exhibits Carter's love of history and unapologetic embrace of idiosyncrasy.
OPPOSITE: An Italian Grand Tour painting hangs over the pine mantel.

Suzanne Kasler

Interior Designer

"I first moved to the South more than 25 years ago, when my husband, John Morris, had to relocate for work. Coming from the Midwest, with a commercial interiors background and a love for contemporary art and architecture, I found it so traditional and overdecorated. But it was the best change for my career. I related to everyone in the South and the way they embrace the idea of home. Being in design here is different from anywhere else in the country—it's such an important part of the culture and permeates everything. Even people who are not in the business are house-proud and take great effort to decorate their homes. I merged my architectural background with the traditional, Southern way of living to create my own take on the style. Mixing antiques with modern art and vintage pieces gives a house an authentic sensibility. And I also really edit. To me, it's all about living with what you love."

Fortuny fabric pillows pick up the leitmotif of glittering metal accents in the living room, which is otherwise dominated by a subtle palette of beiges. A mirror by Mark Evans hangs atop a framed series of maps showing the streets of Paris.

Tell us your favorite things about living in the South.
The focus on the home. The tradition of antiques, which gives the design scene a great foundation. I love Southern hospitality. Southerners love to entertain friends and family in their homes, which is so special. People in the South are also gracious and positive, which creates a welcoming place to live. The weather is wonderful, too.

How do your surroundings enhance your sense of creativity?
The South has so many talented interior and landscape designers and architects. With that kind of engaged community, we have incredible resources, from great design centers and showrooms to vendors and retail stores. Atlanta also has Scott Antique Markets, a monthly flea market. Because of the access to beautiful products and antiques, designers can really take their projects to new heights.

Tell us what you love most about your home.
I had such freedom because I got to be my own client, which meant I could decorate every room exactly the way I wanted to. I worked with architect William T. Baker to reshape the house to my taste and added special details. It originally had a shotgun foyer, but when we shifted the front door so it would be centered on the facade after an addition to the left side of the house, it expanded the space and

created an unusual asymmetrical entryway with the staircase off to the right. It's turned out to be one of my favorite features. I kept most of the footprint and proportion of the original house, so it would be in keeping with the fabric of the neighborhood. Houses should align with the neighbors; it makes such a difference.

What's your entertaining ethos?
When you entertain or have people over, a house absorbs that positive energy. Every year, I host my firm's holiday party at my home. It's not only my favorite event of the year, but also my designers'. I always decorate to the nines for Christmas and use my collection of hotel silver and glassware.

What are a few things every Southern house should have?
Comfortable bedrooms, right down to the pillows and sheets. People who stay at my house often want to order my bedding! Beautiful pieces for entertaining. I have silver from the Connaught Hotel in London, which is my favorite. Flowers, which make a home. I love to set them in a silver ice bucket arranged in a natural way. Places to sit and gather. I bring furniture close together to create intimate settings. A kitchen that is open and comfortable. It's great for entertaining.

Eras blend in the foyer, where a painted 18th-century Louis XVI chair shares space with a 1930s French Moderne gilt parchment covered cabinet, a Picasso lithograph that Kasler found in a shop in Montmartre, and more mirrors by Mark Evans.

Kasler's genius for subtle colorations is on full display in the dining room, which practically glimmers in understated bronzes, golds, and khaki, from gently mirrored moldings to a custom de Gournay wallpaper, to Jansen dining chairs proudly showing off the well-worn original leather.

A vintage library table from the Paris flea market anchors a corner of the living room, complemented by a textured chinoiserie cocktail table and antique Gustavian chairs with serene white cushions.

In a hallway, a pair of Picasso prints are framed in gilt, which echoes the tones of a Louis XVI–style gilt vintage demilune table. OPPOSITE: Ocher accents pop in an ethereal guest bedroom, artfully offset by a series of works by Kris Ruhs.

Kasler worked with architect William T. Baker to center the front door of the house and update its facade with a Regency flair. OPPOSITE: A simple lawn frames the backyard pool and is one of Kasler's (and goldendoodle Murray's) favorite vistas.

McKenzie Dove

Designer and Artist

" I grew up in West Texas, but I married an Alabama man. Michael and I moved to Mountain Brook eight years ago; I fell in love with the landscape and architecture in Birmingham during my first visit and absolutely love living here. We live in a single-story home built in the early 1950s with our one-year-old, Liam, and our dachshund, Sophie."

Refined vintage pieces in pared-down upholstery and a monolithic triptych by Dove sing in her studio, an industrial staging ground sheathed in white.

The interplay between rough-hewn and refined—brick pavers and elaborate vintage gilt consoles—electrifies plaster works by Dove.

What defines Southern living for you and how does your home embody that?
Hospitality. One of my greatest loves is hosting and cooking for friends and family, and I think it's something so appreciated and important in Southern culture. We will often move our dining table into our piano room to accommodate a larger party—I'm not married to any piece of furniture staying in one spot—and my husband is used to me clearing out our den to create space for a dance floor for our annual Christmas party.

How has the region shaped your aesthetic?
Living here has given me a greater appreciation for more traditional objects and furniture. I have been collecting since I was a teen, but the South has provided more opportunities to source china, silver, and antique heirloom pieces from local estate sales.

What's the best thing about your house?
The windows are what I love most about this house. Our house provides a view, both front and back, but still feels secluded, so we've never felt the need to have window treatments in the main areas. And the windows sit low enough for our short-legged dog to sit and look out of them, which, truth be told, is what actually sold my husband on the house.

What makes a house quintessentially Southern?
A china cabinet, heirloom paintings of their children, a Chippendale piece, a Georgian hurricane sconce, a skosh of chinoiserie, lots of blue and white, and a tassel or two—all things I appreciate and have incorporated into our home.

Can you tell us about a tradition that you adopted and why?
Both Michael and I come from creative families and were exposed to music and games. Although our house is not large, we have dedicated a room for music that is really the heart of our home. We often congregate around the piano after dinner, and people will jump in with another instrument or sing along. When my husband and I were dating, we discovered that we were both raised playing the same card game with our families. It's a tradition we still continue in our home. He has yet to beat me, by the way!

If you ever left the South, what would you miss most?
I'd miss the way we show up for and rally around each other in times of need or celebration. There's a culture of generosity that I think is specific to the South. Because of the proximity to everything and the lack of traffic, friends will pop by, which I love. I often come home to sweet notes and gifts just dropped on our porch. It's truly a special way to live.

What's your ethos for entertaining?
Personally, I feel that even in the South, we don't have enough formal sit-down dinners, so I try to make Sunday supper feel special, which has actually turned into a sweet tradition for our family. I make a pot roast and cheesecake that I serve every Sunday at 5 p.m., and friends and family embrace our open-door policy to come by and make a plate. Floral arranging is a favorite art form, as is curating a tablescape with coordinating tapers and fun sets of china. China should be used often!

What are your hosting essentials?
Cast iron, a well-stocked bar, outdoor living spaces, and formal serving pieces are some musts for me. I love a silver champagne bucket and an infused drink dispenser for guests to refill their water at will. And I often prepare martinis ahead of time and keep them in the refrigerator so that they're ready to serve while I plate dinner.

Layers of natural textures like exposed wood floors and woven chairs allow a minimalist approach—which sets off a gallery wall of paper studies and one of Dove's oils—to retain warmth.

Sophie, a dachshund, stands next to a sling chair Dove found outside a Kentucky bar.
Painting electrical boxes and wires white so that they blend into the background
is Dove's way of making lemonade from lemons. OPPOSITE: Greenery thrives in the aptly
named plant room amid a thrift-shop table and vintage iron chairs.

In a sitting room, the reductive palette and keen edit reflect an artist's eye and a yen for sculptural "hero" antiques. Plaster works and painting by Dove.

In the living room, Dove manages to derive a sense of lushness from just a few integral details:
slipcovers with the slightest swish of ruffles, an Asian-inspired cocktail table stripped
of its finish, and a sofa in Schumacher's Verdure Tapestry. OPPOSITE: What looks like a scenic
wallpaper in the dining room is actually a mural hand-painted by Dove herself.

In the primary bedroom, a canopy in Schumacher's Bassano Embroidery
softens estate sale and antique store finds in dark woods.
OPPOSITE: Works by Dove, including a geometric library table, a branch-filled
urn, a chandelier, and painting, take the spotlight in the foyer.

Keith G. Robinson

Gardener and Tastemaker

"**I** live in a historic home, built in 1841 as the centerpiece of a 10,000-acre plantation. It was constructed with an east-west orientation, so the windows capture the light of both the rising sun and dramatic sunsets that fill the receiving room with an amber glow. The house was inhabited by only one family until my tenure, so it has blessedly never undergone any modern renovations. The ancient trees on the property are sentinels of the past and give structure to a garden designed using them as focal points. Additionally, a noteworthy nurseryman and landscape designer installed boxwood parterres on the front of the property in 1837, which still thrive to this day. Native materials used out of necessity and availability yielded original quartz stone walls, which also front the property. It's a curated assemblage that today would be quite costly to replicate. The house's history and the quiet luxury of these elements are what make this place so special."

Madame Cécile Brunner roses spill over a wooden gate and into the first outdoor garden room
Robinson designed on his property, which includes stone-edged perennial beds connected by gravel paths.
The basin is a syrup kettle Robinson unearthed elsewhere on the former plantation.

How has the South shaped your aesthetic?
My family roots are French Creole, and some of my earliest memories are of my paternal grandparents' home in coastal Mississippi, where heirlooms were passed down for generations. From this, I developed an affinity for antique furnishings and accessories to create a sense of history, place, and mystery, and embrace the tradition of storytelling, which is very characteristic of the South.

How does your environment enhance your sense of creativity?
I grew up in the mountains of North Carolina surrounded by beauty: the majesty of the mountains themselves; woods filled with thousands of species of native flowers and shrubs; growing, harvesting, and preparing meals from the land; and a sense of wonder for nature. I try to take the simplest of elements and create something sublime, like when I created large-scale bread boards fashioned out of 170-year-old poplar harvested from a derelict outbuilding on the property. Another time, I discovered milled cedar lumber, long forgotten, drying in the rafters of the barn and used it to build open shelving and plate racks for the kitchen.

Tell us about your favorite Southern tradition.
Having a formal dining room. Growing up in a big family where there were seven at the table (I have three brothers and our maternal grandmother lived with us), we all ate every meal together. Breakfast and lunch were always in the breakfast room, and so was dinner during busy school weeks with varying extracurricular schedules. Saturdays were also casual, but Sundays were *always* in the formal dining room with linens, china, silver flatware, and a beautifully set table. From the age of eight, I foraged in our own garden and the surrounding woodland and fields for flowers from which I created centerpieces for Sunday dinner. Time was spent preparing and presenting the meal, and we took our time enjoying it in a space that felt special. Slowing down and connecting as a family over a lovingly prepared meal—that says *everything* to me about what it means to be Southern.

Why do you think Southern hospitality is so legendary?
Regardless of one's means, Southerners always want to present the absolute best of what they have. Whether that means hosting an event or family gathering when the gardens are in peak bloom or incorporating the sublime umami of foraged chanterelle mushrooms into a special meal, I think that here in the South, we understand and appreciate the magnitude of creating lasting memories and incorporating all the senses into a crescendo that will forever be stamped in the minds of our guests.

What's a Southern rule you love to break?
As we entertain a fair amount, guests generally offer to help clear or clean up or wash dishes. (Much of what we use must be handwashed.) We never allow our guests to help, even if they insist—I have a nightmare story about a guest having a mishap and breaking several dishes! And we don't have a problem having a hard "end time" for a gathering. We wouldn't want folks outstaying their welcome.

What's the quirkiest thing about your house?
Living in a house built in 1841 means that heating and cooling is a challenge. The wavy glass in the original windows is beautiful, but we pay dearly for that beauty!

In an outbuilding that sometimes serves as an entertaining venue, a custom baker's rack holds vintage French and Belgian earthenware jugs. The trestle table was forged from heart pine and poplar boards reclaimed from another outbuilding

Another view of the syrup kettle garden features a Prunus cerasifera 'Thundercloud' plum tree, Fragrant Cloud honeysuckle, and Baptisia alba.

Robinson cut the wood for the kitchen shelves from cedar planks he discovered drying
in the barn rafters. OPPOSITE: A built-in cupboard in the dining room, originally
designed to hold luncheon leftovers, now holds part of Robinson's collection of serving
pieces, which includes antique Limoges and Paris porcelain.

The pelmets that crown the living room curtains are cornices recovered from the barn and date to 1868; Robinson commissioned an artisan to water gild them and paint them with a faux-bois pattern. OPPOSITE: The dining room was built in 1898 to join the main house to the kitchen house. The tablecloth is antique damask; the 19th-century apothecary cabinet is lined in an 18th-century textile and holds more Paris porcelain.

Thad Hayes

Interior Designer and Artist

"I live in a 1955 mashup between a midcentury ranch and a traditional French New Orleans house with my partner, Adam Lippin, and our son, Daniel. For me, history, personal experiences, and what's relevant to you are all part of the design process. Quirk and character play a strong role, too. My home's interiors are an encyclopedia of my life, an accumulation of heirlooms and ideas and elements from my formative years, which were the late 1960s and '70s: my mother's house, midcentury Danish furniture I inherited from my aunt, items I've collected for 50-plus years. There's an emphasis on the kind of easygoing, cool interiors that I obsessed over as a child. My studio is one big culmination of things I love, from the 1930s Flexco rubber floors to a huge Billy Haines horsehead lamp to '70s Zographos club chairs."

A piece by Paul Evans hangs in the studio, which features rubber flooring and walls
paneled in bald cypress with V-grooves. A small bush sculpture by Harry Bertoia sits atop the 1950s
George Nelson for Herman Miller bench.

A fluffy Moroccan shag rug in the living room provides a baseline of texture in an arrangement that includes midcentury modern classics like a Poul Jensen Z armchair and a Noguchi cocktail table. The art is by Richard Serra.

How has the South shaped your aesthetic?
I think that the minimalism I experienced in the '60s and visiting celebrated—but barely furnished—antebellum houses greatly influenced me.

Tell us your favorite things about living in the South.
The climate, which allows for almost year-round entertaining and cooking in the open air with family and friends, a long growing season with fast growth and quick results, and near continual use of our outdoor shower. And family—continuity and familiarity.

Why do you think Southern hospitality is so legendary?
Big stories and big traditions! Historic storytelling is baked into the ethos of my childhood and the South.

Cite five things in your house that make you beam with pride.
The landscape architecture, which includes a wonderful series of gardens I designed and implemented with two friends and colleagues. My cypress-lined studio space, which is separate from the main house and is my workplace and refuge. The cork floors I used throughout the house, which are simple, easy, earthy, and beautiful. The views from the house toward the University Lakes Park—great

sightlines and easy access for walking, biking, or running. And the spa in the studio, which has a porthole window in the shower that looks onto the back garden and a Japanese tub for a serene vibe.

Tell us what every Southern house should have and why.
Breezeways, because they are covered and cool. A porch—also shady and cool, and it functions as a living room that's connected to the landscape and community. A pool, which is refreshing in hot summers and looks great in the landscape. Screen doors and windows that you can leave open most of the year for breezes and circulation. And a courtyard or walled garden because it's classic and fun to be in.

If you had to leave Baton Rouge, what would you miss?
The smells of earth, cypress trees, sweet olive, and camellias; the sound of birds singing; and the food.

What do outsiders get wrong about the region?
I split my time between Louisiana and New York. Half the time, I'm trying to convince Northerners of the joys of the South—the climate and traditions—and the other half, I'm trying to convince Southerners of the joys of different seasons, wide diversity, and possibilities up North!

For the retro-cool kitchen, Hayes had the original St. Charles cabinetry—a favorite of Ludwig Mies van der Rohe and Frank Lloyd Wright—refinished by an auto body shop with chocolate brown paint. OPPOSITE: The moody dining room features a round table with a rich, oil drop finish, chairs by Edward Wormley, and tactile cork floors; the framed Audubon prints complete the mood.

Inspired by the work of Joe D'Urso and Ward Bennett, Hayes devised a desk on wheels that pulls
away to reveal a Japanese soaking tub—allowing both to be centered on the window.
The lamp is by Billy Haines, another influence. OPPOSITE: The studio is also equipped with a bedroom,
complete with built-in cypress shelving and a shuttered closet to store bedding.

Hayes, who began his career as a landscape architect, used local St. Joe brick—the same type used to construct the original house in 1955—for the new exterior walls, patio, and other hardscape.

Mimi McMakin

Interior Designer

"**I** live in a church that was deconsecrated in the 1920s with my wonderfully patient husband, Leroy, two untrainable Jack Russells, and a rotating cast of children, grandchildren, and friends. I grew up next door, in a house called Tree Tops that has since been torn down, and am now the fourth generation of my family to live in the Old Church. Before it was a home, churchgoers came to Sunday service by boat. If sentimentality counts for anything, it overflows for all of us who have lovingly called the Old Church home."

Original lead came windows in the primary bedroom are remnants of the house's past incarnation as a church. The Louis XV–style sofa and armchair, which McMakin inherited from her grandmother, were once heavy and dark, but McMakin painted them white.

The pink porch is named for the soft faded shade on the walls, the result of 40 years' worth of matching and repainting layers and the fading effect of sunlight. A portrait of McMakin's grandmother, a poet, hangs above a hand-carved desk McMakin's great-grandmother brought home from China on a schooner.

Tell us what you love most about living in the South.

So many Southern homes are warm and gracious, which are words that I want to describe all the houses I work on. Southerners are wonderful clients—they are house-proud and often sentimental about the things their mother and father had, and I love working with people who have collections of things that have meaning to them. Southerners are also often wonderful storytellers and make great company.

What does Southern hospitality mean to you?

For me, it's the reason why you don't apologize if your silver isn't polished—it's about the fact that you've loved the collection and are happy to share it, and whoever is enjoying it will feel comfortable, not like you have been working for a week to prepare for their visit—which, as a busy decorator, I don't have time to do! Things need not be perfect to be elegant.

What should every Southern house have?

Plenty of chairs—always two more than you think you can fit—to be pulled up for impromptu conversations.

How do your surroundings shape your point of view?

I am so fortunate to have time to think outdoors with just the sights and sounds of the natural world to inspire me. I don't know how people can think with honking and ambulances screeching in the background. The peacefulness of being surrounded by the quiet voice of nature lets my imagination run free.

Tell us what you treasure most about your home.

My two fiddle-leaf fig trees that have grown up the 12-foot walls of our pink shingled porch—I guess they like it here. The kitchen cabinets: We found them on the street and trompe l'oeiled the fronts of them with shells framing portraits of our children's pets—I look at them every day and they still make me smile. The lead-framed arched windows in our bedroom, still fitted with the old wavy glass that reflects the sunlight and creates a dappled pattern of light across the room. When my grandchildren tell their friends it's OK to roller skate in the house. And watching the expressions of people when they walk into the living room, once the inter-room of the church, now hung with stars and filled with enormous stuffed toy zebras, a giraffe, an alligator, and butterflies—all objects we have collected over the years.

What's a Southern rule you love to break—or just flat-out refuse to follow?

That dogs can't live inside—the lucky ones are even allowed in our bed! Also that children should be seen and not heard—I want my walls to ricochet with happy laughter.

What's the quirkiest thing about your house?

Quirky houses create wonderfully quirky people—and all my favorite people are rife with quirks. Our house isn't like the great houses of Palm Beach. There is nothing gilded about it. It's a monument to romantic chaos.

Tell us about a Southern tradition that you adopted and why.

The Old Church itself. It is very important to me that our children and grandchildren will keep the church close to their hearts and continue to live here for many years to come. My family moved here in 1891, and I feel their footprints where I walk daily. It is a very comforting feeling—I hope it continues for many more generations.

McMakin covered the porch floor in hand-painted Portuguese tiles, an investment she considers one of the best she ever made. For the lamps, she had plain white paper shades painted with an ivy leaf motif. That's Anchovie, a Jack Russell, on the sofa.

The living room, in the old church's nave, is a staging ground for some of McMakin's most treasured furnishings, including a stuffed toy zebra given to her by a friend (she accumulated the giraffes and tigers to keep it company) and Balinese umbrellas she had wired to cast light down onto the seating area. The alligator cocktail table is a prototype of one she had made for a client.

CLOCKWISE FROM TOP LEFT: Hand-painted house signs lead the way. The coquina walkway
is edged in Bahamian conch shells. A ceramic frog shares space with porcelain plates,
a painting by McMakin, and a pocket planter she fills with garden greens. Antique fishing rods lean
in a corner of the sitting room. OPPOSITE: Turtle and Anchovie guard the entrance to the pink
porch, which also serves as the main entrance to the house.

Ann Mashburn

Fashion Designer

"We live in a Georgian-style house built in the 1930s and designed by architect Francis Palmer Smith. It feels romantically Southern to me—the garden, the big front hall, and architectural elements that feel kind of stately—but the house isn't big, and I love that. I call it 'petite grand.' I'm a Southerner by marriage (I'm originally from all over the Midwest). My husband and business partner, Sid, is from a small town outside Jackson, Mississippi. We met in New York City and moved to Atlanta in 2007 to start our fashion company. Two of our five daughters—Louisa, 31, and Harriet, 27—have a progressive motor neuro disease and will always live with us. It's a multigenerational household!"

In the living room, a ping-pong table topper ushers a Louis XV–style table into a more casual incarnation; a Volta mobile hanging above catches the vibe. Fanny, a dachshund, hogs the ball.

Tell us a few things you love most about your house.
It sits up on a hill like a white cupcake, and at any time of the day, at least one room has extraordinary light with shadows that make me stop to take yet another iPhone photo. On the first floor, the front windows are double height and fitted with old glass. Every time I come up the driveway, I appreciate their wavy ripples. There are three porthole windows in the house, and the woman who lived in the house before us added a porthole to her office door, a quirk that I love. And I love that you can see all the way through to the back garden as soon as you walk in the front door.

How does your home embody Southern living?
We lean into the fact that there are four adults living in our house together. It is a very American idea that your grown children ought to leave for good. When we go to Italy, it is super inspiring to me to see multiple generations living in the same household—it's much more common in Europe than it is here. When my girls were diagnosed with a progressive disease in their mid-20s, I realized that we were all going to live together forever, and I had better learn how to make it great. It is pretty Southern to embrace tragedy and make it beautiful.

How and why do you entertain?
I have a big family, so I entertain a lot just by feeding them. My oldest daughter lives in town with her husband, and with Louisa and Harriet,

it's an instant full house. Even if it's just the six of us eating on a Sunday evening, it feels like a party. I love to have people over at the last minute—I am a better casual entertainer. I *did* throw a pretty great wedding with the ceremony in the front yard and reception in the back. It was very homey and sweet. I was completely in over my head, and it felt very much like a barn raising, with my friends all helping on the day with all the last-minute details. It all felt very Southern in spirit—even if it was more about my doing everything last minute and being a little bit delusional in what I could accomplish independently.

How has the South shaped your aesthetic?
I have shared a home with a Southerner since I was 23, when we both lived in a loft on Duane Street in Tribeca. Sid had this aunt who (randomly and clandestinely) gave him some of the inherited family silver. It wasn't much, but he must have been the favorite nephew, because she wanted him to have it. We used that silver recklessly. I think maybe that was the beginning of my adopting the very Southern habit of using "the good stuff" every day.

Can you tell us about a favorite Southern tradition?
Don't call, just show up—and bring some food with you! My husband's best friend, another Mississippian (and godfather to our oldest daughter) always just stops by. This ease of knowing you are always welcome is very Southern to me. For Sid, it is completely normal, but my girls and I are still surprised—and charmed—by it!

A Gustavian-style settee with the last throes of its original painted finish still intact gracefully grounds the foyer beneath antique candle sconces and a simple mirror.

Classic roll arm sofas upholstered in a sunwashed shade of pink linen give a white-and-greige color scheme some happy punctuation, while a modernist vintage Italian cocktail table adds a contemporary note.

Clean geometries dominate the kitchen, which was designed by the house's previous owner, interior designer Kay Douglass, but delicately veined marble surfaces and a beadboard hood keep things from veering too sterile. OPPOSITE: Saarinen tables of varying size hopscotch down a sightline from a sitting area to the dining room, bridging two spaces where curving antiques also feel right at home.

In the primary bedroom, shapely Barcelona chairs are an era-blurring match for an antique Louis XV–style bed with an undulating profile.

In the primary bathroom, treetop views and a flood of natural light are the major design notes. OPPOSITE: An antique chinoiserie canopy bed is the highlight of a guest room where a well-edited selection of antiques gains modernist edge thanks to bare floors and a minimum of decoration on the walls.

Matthew Monroe Bees

Interior Designer

"I grew up in L.A.—that's 'lower Alabama' for those in the know—so I'm Southern by birth. I have a strong bond to my upbringing—so much so that I was unable to follow the usual design route to New York City. I felt the need to leave Alabama to expand my education, but I couldn't leave the South, so I relocated to Charleston in 2009. My home is a typical mid-19th-century Charleston Single. It was converted into a shop with a shopkeeper's apartment upstairs as this stretch of King Street became more commercial and less residential. I live in the old shopkeeper's apartment. It's just me and my seven-year-old doodle, Presley—he's a Southern boy, too, from Tupelo, Mississippi, just like his namesake."

In the primary bedroom, art by Frank Phillips hangs atop a Gracie Studio folding screen installed on the wall.

How has the South shaped your aesthetic?
I grew up with a very interiors-focused grandmother who owned and managed a large cattle farm in Crenshaw County, Alabama. When I was just starting to develop my own style, architects like Bobby McAlpine and Greg Tankersley were showing us how to rethink the Southern interior. Gone were the rooms of my youth with their heavy American Empire furniture; they were replaced with lighter European antiques and linen upholstery. And I always say my *real* education in Southern decorating began when I moved to Charleston. We have a unique way of blending old and new that gives life to our interiors.

What is Southern living to you?
Our lives revolve around social activities. We entertain on a grand scale in the South, and our houses are designed to accommodate that. My dining room can seat 10 comfortably; however, if I set up a buffet, open the doors, and arrange a bar on the piazza (what we call a porch in Charleston), I can entertain 60-plus people.

Why do you think Southern hospitality is so legendary?
We'll use any reason to throw a party! For me, it always begins with deciding what I'm using on my table or buffet. Many of these pieces are family heirlooms or something I've scored at an auction. Then there's the food, with many of the recipes also handed down. And every party begins with the invitation: I treat my stationery vendor like a member of the family. I can't tell you how many times my grandmother sent her regrets for an event because she didn't approve of the invitation!

What's a Southern rule you flat-out refuse to follow?
I have no rugs. After I stripped the heart pine floors of a very red stain, they were so beautiful that I simply whitewashed and sealed them. This caused my original flooring contractor to quit because he could not conceive whitewashing heart pine floors, so I found a younger guy who got what I was trying to accomplish. Once completed, I left them bare, and I love them.

What's a Southern tradition you've adopted?
I make my bed every day with pressed linens, and I never leave a dirty dish in the sink—lessons from my paternal grandparents. My grandfather was a navy man, so making your bed was just what you did when you woke up each day. And my grandmother used to say that if she died in her sleep, she'd be so embarrassed for someone to come in and find a mess of dirty dishes in the kitchen!

Tell us five of your favorite things about living in the South.
Our social seasons: In Charleston, it's all about the spring festivals that lead up to Spoleto; in Mobile, it's Mardi Gras, which begins the Wednesday before Thanksgiving and runs until Ash Wednesday. Our families, and the way we keep those ties strong through traditions. Our beaches—they never seem to be far away—and our mountains, because the minute the heat sets in, there's always someone's grandmother with a fabulous mountain home and an open invite. And the food: From barbecue stands to James Beard Award–winning restaurants, we have it all—and it keeps getting better.

Trompe-l'oeil millwork with a Regency inflection by artist Cristina Pepe meets the heft of custom interior doors with whimsy and charm. The bergère is covered in Mellier Plaid by Schumacher.

In the living room, a graphic zebra-print rug and geometric pillows in Cubist by Miles Redd for Schumacher give an au courant update to stately antiques and fulsome balloon shades in Bagan fabric by Celerie Kemble for Schumacher.

Faux-bois wallpaper from Thibaut gives dimension to the living room, where chairs that once belonged to Mario Buatta mingle with an antique secretary. OPPOSITE: A sunny lemon yellow—inspired by the dining room at Monticello—enlivens the kitchen.

Schumacher's Incomparable Moiré fabric creates a broodingly glamorous
backdrop on foyer walls. OPPOSITE: Bird and Thistle wallpaper by Brunschwig & Fils
turns the guest bedroom into an enchanted forest.

Jeannette Whitson

Interior Designer

"I was born in the South, although I lived in many different places growing up and again after I was married. My husband and I lived in Jakarta, Indonesia, for four years, but Southern indoctrination is strong; like sea turtles, we eventually found ourselves back on familiar shores. Around 2012, when I returned to the South, the housing market was very tight, and after a year of trying to find a historic house to no avail, I decided to build a new 'old' house. Architect Roman Hudson and I designed the house to look like a Georgian stone cottage that had been added onto over time. I love the stone cottages of the Cotswolds—I'm especially drawn to the patina of the local limestone formed there when the world was submerged in a shallow sea and the remnants of prehistoric crustaceans, ammonites, and reptiles melded with the silt and clay. Luckily, Tennessee has a similar geological history."

In the living room, French armchairs re-covered in cowhide face an antique tufted leather sofa that the former antiques dealer bought in England. A fireplace surround in rough-hewn stone adds another layer of texture.

Whitson loves to bring outdoor elements—like the mushroom garden statue and English lantern—into her home to blur the lines between interior and exterior. The custom stair rail was inspired by Chinese Chippendale furniture.

What gives your house its character?

Having been an antiques dealer for 25 years, I embrace imperfection: Dents, scratches, and blemishes here and there only make a piece more interesting. I used restoration glass in all the windows and doors, and the slight bubbles scatter the light and diffuse it in a unique way that adds depth and visual interest. Authentic materials like copper, cedar shake, real clapboard siding, and limestone lend a sense of timelessness as well. I bought a batch of reclaimed English sidewalks and used them for the terraces around the house. They came with all the markings that thousands of people walking on them would reveal, along with embedded fossils and deep-rooted mosses. Almost all of the lighting in the house is antique, with carriage lanterns over the kitchen island and dining room table. A low stone pig trough is now a sink in the butler's pantry, and an old head of Pan spout from the garden now spits water into a lead garden urn in the powder room. I am not a minimalist!

What does Southern living mean to you?

The lifestyle has a slower pace, always involves family and friends, and has a deep connection to the outdoors. When designing or renovating houses, I am always trying to open them up to the outside and create spaces that rarely need artificial light. Our house is built in a U shape with a central terrace in the back onto which every interior room opens. In our climate, that space can be used almost year-round, and even when the doors are closed, the connection to nature is strong. I've collected garden antiques for years, and they flow in and out of the house, blurring the boundary between indoors and out. We had a rare snowfall the other day, and sitting in my kitchen was like being in a snow globe.

How has the South shaped your aesthetic?

My mother and grandmother were keen gardeners, and I grew up with fresh flowers always around. As a child, my day started with a slam of the back door as my brother and I went off to the creek to catch animals and build forts. We were only told to be home before dark. Can you imagine? Having hours to contemplate snails in a creek bed and make place settings with rocks in our makeshift fort? Creativity is born in nature.

What's a Southern rule you love to break?

I've broken a lot of rules in my time, but the strict Southern code of thank-you notes I find especially brutal. When giving a wedding or baby gift, I always include a little card I had printed that says, "In order to free you for more creative use of your time, we request you omit the customary personal letter of thanks."

179

The library, swathed completely in rich shades of blue, features a tented ceiling covered in an *Indienne*-inspired floral fabric by Jasper and a custom sectional upholstered in Schumacher's plush Gainsborough velvet.

A pinch-pleat curtain disguises storage in the butler's pantry. Whitson installed the porthole on the door to allow sunlight to reach interior spaces and create a sightline from the other end of the house. OPPOSITE: Whitson expanded the kitchen to create a "keeping room," complete with a breakfast nook that can seat 12.

An outdoor lantern illuminates the kitchen, while a rustic-yet-refined steel hood helps to incorporate it seamlessly into the shipshape furnishings, which include French rattan stools and brass hardware.

Whitson found the mud room's slate sink in a Nashville salvage yard.
OPPOSITE: Reclaimed sidewalk pavers from England set the mood on the screened porch,
where they are instantly elevated by antique French rattan-and-bamboo seating.

Elizabeth Damrich

Creative Director and Designer

"I live with my husband, Michael, and our two children, Gigi and John Monroe, in the Rapier House, an 1885 Greek Revival residence in the Oakleigh Garden Historic District, a neighborhood in Mobile that's on the National Register of Historic Places. At heart, I'm a true romantic—and I blame that all on the South. I first fell in love with Greek Revival architecture in my hometown of Athens, Alabama, where I was lucky to grow up surrounded by beautiful, well-preserved buildings from the past. I could name the order of columns before I could say a sentence! I love the strength and beauty of Greek Revival symmetry set against the wild landscape. It's what drew me to the Rapier House and its Ionic columns. Ionic is the feminine order and I just love what that represents."

The historic Rapier House was rebuilt in 1909 with a Greek Revival facade after a fire damaged the original 1885 structure. The double sphinx sculpture is a Provençal antique.

What defines Southern living for you?

For me, it's about living well and living thoughtfully. There is a gentleness and a graciousness built into the spirit of the houses here. You feel it in the design—the higher ceilings and tall windows that give you space to breathe and create, the curtains that puddle onto the floor in a generous way, heirlooms reminding you of where you came from. It's finding comfort in positioning your chair just right on the porch so that you can sunbathe in the afternoon with your eyes closed and then repositioning it later that night to sit with family and a glass of wine while the cicadas lull you to sleep.

Describe your approach to entertaining.

We have had some great parties in this house. I feel like she was built for it and really beams when she is full of people and music. I love a sense of ease built into entertaining—even if I'm wearing some fancy gown, I'm likely barefoot. I love candlelight, serving pizza on my nice silver, and endless amounts of champagne.

What comes to mind when you think of a Southern house?

The scent of freshly cut grass or jasmine wafting in from the garden. Large, old windows that open from the ground up. A tray with glasses, a pitcher, and cheese straws ready to be served. Distant conversation and laughter coming from the porch. Silver cups and vases that have been passed down for generations. A box of handwritten recipes or a box stashed with last year's Christmas cards. A radio on low with the sound of college football.

Are there any Southern rules that you refuse to follow?

"No white after Labor Day" or any other narrow-minded fashion rule—I like to push the envelope and don't mind ruffling the feathers of people who stay within the box. Never leaving the house without a full face of makeup is another: My grandmother would be disappointed, but I love a fresh face. And keeping a formal living room where children are not welcome: Just like we should wear our nice clothes, we also need to enjoy our furniture. I want my kids to know what it means to take care of things and love them from an early age.

What makes Southern houses so special?

Quirk is one of the best things about Southern homes—particularly historic ones. Nothing is necessarily "en suite"—I have closets of clothes throughout the house. It's OK to have to walk a little bit! I also love to switch up where we eat dinner, so we often carry a café table around the house to enjoy meals from a different viewpoint. And we don't have an official "playroom" for the kids. Instead, I like to have pockets of toys hidden throughout the house so it isn't overwhelming, and I'm not forced to sit in a single-use space filled with them all day.

Bare floors and clean white walls in the foyer are a pared-down foundation for a Julie Neill plaster chandelier and graphic tablecloth made from Even Stripe Indoor/Outdoor fabric by Caroline Z. Hurley for Schumacher. The iron chair and shell mirror are antiques Damrich picked up in New Orleans.

Original dentil moldings crown white-painted millwork in the "tapestry room."
OPPOSITE: The Aubusson tapestry that gives the room its name is a romantic foil for an
angular slipcovered sofa and a low-slung cocktail table.

Damrich calls this the "pink room" for the barely-there shade (Farrow & Ball's Dimity) that covers the walls and imbues the space with a flattering warm glow, especially at night. OPPOSITE: Several seating options and plenty of places to set down a drink make the room a shoe-in for entertaining.

A fragment of a Zuber scenic wallpaper is framed in the foyer; the antique iron chair once graced the halls of the Soniat House Hotel in New Orleans. OPPOSITE: In the guest room, curtains and a bed canopy in Schumacher's Prestwick Wool Satin (the latter trimmed in Heraldic Trim by Happy Menocal for Schumacher) make for a cosseting refuge. The bedspread is in Incomparable Moiré by Schumacher.

John Pope

Antiques Dealer

"I was born in Missouri, attended Savannah College of Art and Design, and decided to stay in the Lowcountry and move to Charleston. I live in a building originally constructed in 1849 as the Vigilant Fire Company, one of Charleston's leading fire department stations. It later became the Maritime Union Hall, then a grocery store. It turned residential in the 1950s, and tile floors and classical woodwork were installed. The city of Charleston, with its history, architecture, and connection to nature, still holds a sense of place and soul. And the Lowcountry as a natural environment is unparalleled: From salt marshes to coastal waterways, it is a backdrop that constantly surrounds us here. Rising and falling tides, migrating birds, and the sunrises and sunsets are a calming force in a busy world."

In the foyer, a framed 19th-century Turkish servant's jacket hangs amid collected objects including embossed metal tea trays and a specimen marble sampler.

The living room, with a
charming mix that includes
a 19th-century Scottish
convex mirror, 18th- and
19th-century Chinese
and Islamic pottery (on the
mantel), and easeful
1970s rattan armchairs,
reflects the peripatetic eye
of a connoisseur.

Tell us what Southern living means to you.
Entertaining and hospitality. They influence our design and decoration, especially in creating flexible spaces with lots of extra seating that's easy to pull up and rearrange: stools, benches, garden seats. I usually leave my dining table small for a more intimate dinner, but it can expand to seat 12. In the winter, having lunch or dinner in front of the fire at the marble-top table in the living room is a highlight. My bar is always set, stocked, and ready, with everything at my fingertips. I just add ice to the bucket and cut some fruit and I'm always ready to entertain.

How has the region shaped your aesthetic?
Southern homes are warm, welcoming, and inviting, with plenty of collected objects that are rich with history. I like my home to tell stories of my travels and things I've accumulated along the way. Most of my belongings invoke memories of my adventures.

Tell us about a few of your favorite things in your house.
My collection of grand tour souvenirs is my longest running. It's turned into a bit of a cabinet of curiosities with antique classical objects, bugs, shells, and dried leaves reminding me of trips or events in my life. I also love the paneled woodwork in the house and the tile floors installed in the 1950s. Though not documented, some historians believe that they were designed by iconic local architect Albert Simons, whose office was just down the street. The carved cornices, paneled chimney piece, and bookshelves were all beautifully crafted in Charleston.

Why do you think Southern hospitality is so legendary?
I think Southerners are truly inquisitive and interested in meeting new people. They're always willing to host and entertain and share their love of the South.

What should every Southern house have and why?
Options for entertaining! An array of silver, china, glassware, and linens. Setting a beautiful table makes everyone happy.

How do you know a house is Southern?
Open the pantry—if there are grits, you're in the South!

Why is it important to have quirk or character in a home?
Southern homes can be formal yet relaxed, elegant but not staid. They don't take themselves too seriously, and they'll mix the high and the low in the same space, which allows you to be surrounded by beautiful objects and still feel comfortable. Some of the floor tiles in my house are loose—they click and clatter. I've considered having them fixed, but there's something charming about the noise. I can tell where my dog is by the sound of the clacks in the hallway.

Geometric 1970s Marianna von Allesch lamps frame shuttered windows, a 1950s French abstract painting, and a plaster maquette in the manner of neoclassical French sculptor Jean-Antoine Houdon.

A Napoleon II rosewood armchair covered in a jewel-toned moiré is sumptuously electrifying
near a framed Art Deco pen-and-ink drawing and a kilim-covered Parsons bench.
OPPOSITE: A 19th-century French portrait of a North African man takes pride of place in the den,
surrounded by 18th-century English Delftware and Indian and Moroccan tea trays.

CLOCKWISE FROM TOP LEFT: Pope's burgeoning collection of Grand Tour souvenirs. Iranian pottery and heirloom rosaries sit on an Indian tray table. A Maison Jansen side table holds military epaulets. The Saarinen tulip table was once in Pope's father's office. OPPOSITE: In the primary bedroom, a woven Guatemalan ikat dresses the canopy of an 18th-century English bed, which in turn is outfitted with a lush Suzani.

Kristin Ellen Hockman

Interior Designer

"In 2016, my husband and I were living in New York City and booked a last-minute weekend getaway to Charleston. We instantly fell in love with the town: the architecture, the accessibility, the size, the proximity to the beach—everything. We went back to New York, quit our jobs, moved down here, and the rest is history! Our home, Gippy, was built in 1852 in a Greek Revival style, with gardens said to be designed by a famous landscape architect, Loutrel Briggs. Originally part of a plantation, the property was purchased by the Roosevelt family in the 1920s to use as a hunting lodge. It is listed on the National Register of Historic Places and is one of the last remaining examples of 19th-century Greek Revival architecture in Berkeley County."

Hockman repurposed an old tablecloth to make slipcovers for the Gustavian chairs in the dining room; the walls are painted in Pale Powder from Farrow & Ball.

A path framed by boxwood parterres leads through an array of magnolia trees,
crepe myrtles, live oaks, and tea olive. OPPOSITE: The gardens are rumored to have been designed
by Loutrel Briggs, a prominent Southern landscape architect in the early 20th century.

Floors in the main hallway are original heart pine and date to 1852; the 19th-century inlaid table is Italian.

What does Southern living mean to you and how does your home embody that ideal?
To me, it's about having a house that makes your guests want to stay a little longer and let their hair down, where all pretentiousness is left at the doorstep. But it's also about not brushing the South's past under the rug. That means acknowledging the painful history of our house, which was built by enslaved artisans. It is incredibly important to us that we honor the original architecture of our home, never change anything that was built using enslaved labor, and educate our guests on how this home came to be.

Tell us five of your favorite things about living in the South.
I love the stillness—the way I can hear the train go by during the night and the cicadas singing in the summertime. I love how our neighbors have welcomed us with open arms and have become our extended family. I love the distinct smell of tea olive wafting through the air when it's in bloom; it's the most magnificent scent there is. I love how there's not a sense of urgency here, how the slower pace puts you at ease. I love how I can sit on the front porch with my daughter and watch the Spanish moss blow in the wind while a summer thunderstorm rolls in.

Why do you think Southern hospitality is so legendary?
Having good manners is a way of life here. Always "yes ma'am," "no ma'am," "let me hold the door for you," and "can I help you with that?" It is ingrained in Southerners to always show respect. But it's important to remember that it must be reciprocal. Southerners have a sense of pride for who they are and where they come from, so if you want to be welcomed with open arms, you have to respect that, too. If someone comes down here and starts complaining to a native Southerner about how much better life is in the Midwest or the North or wherever they may be from, well then—bless their heart!

Can you tell us about a tradition that you adopted?
An open-door policy. Because we are stewards of a historic home, it is our duty to make sure we are always available for anyone wanting to learn more about the property. Every once in a while, we have someone show up at our doorstep who has some sort of connection to Gippy, and it's always so exciting to invite them in for a tour and hear their stories and memories of our house.

What makes a house quintessentially Southern?
A few telltale signs: There's faint blue paint on the porch ceiling, Duke's mayonnaise in the fridge, and a host constantly asking if you would like anything to eat or drink (homemade, of course!). Bonus points if there's a Boykin spaniel asleep on a dog bed that perfectly complements the decor.

What's a Southern rule you flat-out refuse to follow?
Monograms on everything! We have a pair of monogrammed hand towels, but that is it. I do not need my initials on my duvet or everything hanging in my (or my daughter's) closet.

In the family room, a plainspoken paper lantern pulls antiques like a 19th-century Queen Anne–style English daybed and a neoclassical giltwood mirror firmly into the present day. OPPOSITE: In the formal living room, curving silhouettes—an antique camelback sofa and a neoclassical recamier—sit under the watchful eyes of 18th-century portraits of Charles III of Spain and Maria Amalia of Saxony.

The kitchen has been
thoroughly modernized
with a La Cornue
range and a deep apron
sink; the walls are
covered in French Grey
from Farrow & Ball.

Daughter Astrid plays in her bedroom at a child-size table Hockman painted
and decorated with a Greek key motif. OPPOSITE: The room is
anchored by a painted Directoire daybed for which Hockman created a simple—
and sweet—canopy from a Chelsea Textiles gingham.

Michael Devine & Thomas Burak

Textile Designer and Interior Designer

"**T**homas and I live in a Dutch Colonial–style stone house in Central Virginia designed by noted Charlottesville architect Milton Grigg and built in 1950 with several later additions, one inspired by Monticello. I'm from Illinois and Thomas is from upstate New York, and we spent most of our adult lives in New York City until Zillow brought us to the South. We had spent two years looking for a place in Connecticut to no avail; one day, I searched Virginia on a lark, and now we've been here for five years."

Burak and Devine reverse-engineered the dining room's crystal chandelier—originally electrified—to hold tapers instead of lightbulbs. Salvaged black slate and white marble floors complete the elegant effect.

Tell us your favorite things about living in the South.
The extended gardening season, which means that I can be doing something in the garden twelve months a year. (Thomas isn't nearly as thrilled about this perk as I am.) The great group of friends we've made. The nearby restaurants and local farms. Historic houses that we visit often for inspiration. And the natural beauty of the area we live in.

Cite five things in your house that make you beam with pride.
The layout of the house is great both for weekend guests and for large parties. The house was built using a lot of historic mantel, doors, and light fixtures, which really speak to us, like the salvaged black slate and white marble floors in the dining room and the foyer. The sunroom with its eastern exposure is perfect for breakfast when it's bathed in sunlight. The hand-painted tiles in the kitchen are from the marvelous French firm Ponchon, the same company that provided the tiles for Monet's kitchen at Giverny.

What defines Southern living for you?
Graciousness and generosity are the definition of our experiences living in Virginia. We really use our house for entertaining, and I think because of that, it has a welcoming and comfortable feel to it. We have lots of dinner parties, and we use them as a chance to show our creativity—setting the table is always stretching the imagination.

How and why do you entertain?
We entertain for the pleasure of the company. We love entertaining in different areas of the house: Small dinners in winter are in the library; larger dinners are in the dining room, which is only lit by candlelight and a fireplace; and in the summer, we use either the garden or the sunroom with its view of the outdoors.

What does every Southern house need?
Cheese straws for impromptu visits. Bourbon, the favored drink in our area. Great glassware to serve all that bourbon in. An Edna Lewis cookbook for really great Southern fare. Lots of vases for all the flowers from the garden.

What's a Southern rule you refuse to follow?
I don't eat pimento cheese. Thomas does love it, though.

What's most intriguing about the houses in the South?
The quirkiness is what gives these houses their character. Ours was built over time and has some things that baffle us, but we love it all the more for the uniqueness of these things.

If you had to leave the South, what would you miss the most and why?
Our house, which really is perfection for us, and our friends, because a perfect house is nearly impossible to find (trust us on this) and friends are precious and irreplaceable.

What do people get wrong about the South?
The food. It's not all fried and collard greens! We have a diverse and vibrant food and wine scene that does not fit the stereotypical idea of Southern food.

The library, which also doubles as a dining room for intimate gatherings, contains a wealth of titles collected over decades, with topics ranging from antiques and gardening to French literature. The 18th-century Flemish verdure tapestry and antique Swedish chairs ensure a cozy refinement.

The living room walls are gently dappled in a gray lime wash (Caviar from Ressource Paints) to create an atmospheric envelope for antiques like an Italian armchair covered in tiger stripe velvet and a gilt French mirror. OPPOSITE: The mirror-backed trellis visually multiplies a collection of blue-and-white porcelain.

An antique neoclassical chair Burak found in Paris is upholstered in a textile from
Devine's fabric line, Michael Devine Ltd. OPPOSITE: A vintage tufted
chaise holds court in a corner of the library, where Burak and Devine's collection
of Russian Impressionism paintings also hang.

Bobby McAlpine
Architect

"I designed my house with my partner, Blake Weeks. It's steeply appointed with seemingly disparate oddities and finds from travel and things trotted out from the attic. Some are ravaged, on the brink of ruin, and some are in fine condition. They're like guests at our tables and on our porches. Most of the upholstery and drapery fabrics are made up of old Irish linen tablecloths mismatched and monogrammed by God knows who. Some of the fabrics are threadbare and surviving through elbow patches. In the entry, with its transporting cross section of antique treasures, the shabbiness of the wood walls and the cooling sleekness of the marble slab floors come together to exemplify the breadth of the things I'm passionate about. The push and pull between theatrical scale and the compressive low alcoves also speaks to that inertia and ascension that I love when paired."

McAlpine designed the house to descend to the street on a series of terraces, complete with basalt steps.

How do you define Southern living?
Porches, breezeways, and outbuildings are standard fare in this temperate climate. Decoration can be eccentric and, at the least, eclectic.

What do you love most about where you live?
The people and the characters. Heat and rural isolation tend to brew up the best of the best. People in the South are glad to see you and want good things for you. It also seems the easiest place to think up something and get it done—there is not a lot of bureaucracy in place to stop you. And, certainly, eccentricity and patina are part of the diet here.

How does the environment enhance creativity?
That heat, isolation, and boredom create a roux in us that in turn fosters great storytelling through literature, art, and design.

Tell us five things every Southern house should have and why.
Dogs—I wouldn't trust anyone who didn't have one. An enormous table, because you could live your life at a table. A hundred mismatched chairs—the personifications of all the people we love. A well-stocked pantry, so there is no reason to leave. An interior with a strong point of view, because it edifies your take on the world.

Why is Southern hospitality so famous?
Small towns and rural locations don't provide us with restaurants and venues to help us entertain. Our homes become our way of sharing everything and everyone, and all the refinements that trail that reality show up here in the South.

What's your entertaining ethos?
Inviting friends to stay for a long weekend is worth a year of dinner dates in getting to know someone. Great guest rooms are a way of celebrating the visitor.

Can you tell us about a tradition passed down to you that you adopted and why?
My house is always clean, straight, and ready to receive anyone.

Are there any Southern rules you prefer to ignore?
It is rare that I will ever put a door in the middle of a house where I prefer a window instead, as it is the best seat for viewing the inside.

Why is quirk or character so important to Southern houses?
A gap in the teeth or a lazy eye is easy to walk toward. Perfection is repellent and non-inclusive.

Give us a few words that sum up the South.
These go for the house, too: Honest, forthright, celebrative, theatrical, eclectic.

A soaring custom bay window dominates the living room and dining room, where an eclectic blend of antiques and *objets*—stone eagles, a sculpted bear head, a ravaged wooden bench—cast atmospheric shadows.

The space blends muscular interior architecture with utilitarian materials (like a cantilevered steel bedroom loft, walls paneled in thin cedar strips, and a brick inglenook) and refined antiques (such as pairs of gilt consoles and lanterns).

The soaring curtains and upholstery on custom sofas were made from antique Irish linen tablecloths. OPPOSITE: McAlpine hid HVAC vents and outlets in subtle gaps between the marble flooring and interior walls. The mushrooms are antique wooden sculptures painted white by his partner, Blake Weeks.

A monolithic staircase made from lacquered wood layered over steel bares no delineation between tread and riser and climbs three stories through the center of the house. OPPOSITE: Diaphanous gauze drapes help draw the line between public and private spaces.

ABOVE, FROM LEFT: Scrolling gilt antiques juxtapose marble in one of a pair of
his-and-his primary bathrooms. A Michael Marlowe painting—one of a triptych—
adds a note of gentle color to a mostly white guest room. OPPOSITE: Stacked firewood
creates a naturally artful backdrop for a custom headboard and bedside table.

Thomas Jayne

Interior Designer and Decorative Arts Historian

"My husband, Rick Ellis, and I split our time between a loft in New York and an apartment in a Creole townhouse in New Orleans—the smallest in the French Quarter, built circa 1830. We redid the interiors in the 19th-century Creole taste with the help of the late architect Frank W. Masson. We were attracted by Southern hospitality, especially the food, and the architecture. Rick is a food stylist and historian and has one of the finest and largest collections of Southern cookbooks in the world—over 5,000 volumes. All our closest family live in the South: My cousin and goddaughters are in New Orleans, and all of Rick's relations are scattered throughout the South. There are six apartments in our building, and we're close with our neighbors, who all love food. We have a parlor floor with a balcony that we occasionally host parties on. Often, leftovers are passed along through the courtyard."

In the living room, subtle pink walls (in Benjamin Moore's Marry Me) are a warm
backdrop for a collection of Thomas Frye mezzotints, 19th-century American gondola chairs,
and a clean-lined mirror with a graphic red frame.

The courtyard garden, dotted with potted palms, is an outdoor venue where Jayne and his husband often entertain with neighbors.

What are your favorite things about living in the South?
In no particular order: The rich, shared cuisine of the South, which unifies it. Camellias—I love the subtropical landscape here and especially these blooms. Family and friends: Showing up for events and proximity to them is important. The light, which has an impressionist quality. And the Mississippi: With interests in farming and timber, my family has strong connections to the whole stretch of the river from Muscatine, Iowa, to New Orleans.

How has the region shaped your point of view?
It's hard to say exactly, but it definitely has something to do with tradition. Old-fashioned manners still prevail. Reciprocal dinner parties, time to talk, and the regular use of courtesy titles—Miss, Mr., Dr.—all come to mind. I think we use more silver and porcelain here—whenever I see a silver beaker, I think of the South. And we cannot live without white tablecloths.

What does Southern hospitality mean to you?
Southerners invest time and treasure in entertaining on a scale unlike any other place in the country, and they keep in practice. When Southerners give a party, they don't have to run around last minute buying plates at Crate & Barrel.

What are the most special pieces in your house?
The custom mural we commissioned for the living room from de Gournay, inspired by illustrations by C.H. DeWitt from *The Story of the Mississippi*, one of my favorite childhood books. The old doors with their hardware, which we were able to salvage despite a 1960s remodel that sadly resulted in the loss of much of the house's original detailing; along with the windows, they created a historic core for the renovated rooms. The original floors, which immediately convey antiquity. My decadent slab marble shower. And our "real" art, including pieces by Albert Hadley, Sally Mann, Hunt Slonem, and Don Bachardy, because you cannot have a good room without a work of art.

How do you entertain?
There are many occasions to celebrate, especially with Mardi Gras. Things that help: Silver in the kitchen drawer, a large set of white and gold china, and lots of places to sit.

List five things every Southern house should have.
Wicker chairs, ceiling fans, curtains, a Mardi Gras mask, and maybe a flask.

How can you tell you're in a Southerner's house?
Any of these would clue me in: family portraits or paintings of magnolias on the walls, Herend figurines, bowls of spiced pecans, a collection of sun hats, social stationery, or a well-used dining room.

What's a Southern rule you love to break?
I like to wear seersucker after Labor Day!

What do outsiders get wrong about the region?
Since, legally, I am a Yankee by birth and genealogy, it is polite that I forgo this question.

To create the parlor's pièce de résistance— a charming mural wallpaper rooted in a sense of place—Jayne commissioned de Gournay to create panels based on a favorite childhood book, *The Story of the Mississippi*, by C.H. DeWitt.

Jayne restored the parlor room ceilings to their original beams and boards.
The furniture is meant to be moved and reconfigured at will—an old
Southern custom that's perfect for parties. OPPOSITE: German woodblock prints
featuring carnival characters reflect Jayne's love of Mardi Gras.

The primary bedroom's wallpaper—Butterfly Chintz by Adelphi Paper
Hangings—is a hand-blocked copy of an antique French paper in
the collection at Colonial Williamsburg. OPPOSITE: Jayne counteracted the
lilting print with an Audubon print of a vulture.

Angie Hranowsky
Interior Designer

"I live with my son, Sasha, and our cat, Rocco—my daughter, Loulou, 21, is away at college—in a modern house that I designed and had built from the ground up. I worked with architect Johnny Tucker to draw my ideas and help me bring them to fruition. My house is inspired by the things I love most, including elements of our local vernacular. The layout is informal, with glass walls that flood the interiors with light and a long, wraparound porch that has welcomed many a hang. My yard is a tropical oasis of palms and bamboo, and the house itself is built of cypress, which is indigenous to South Carolina."

An Ingo Maurer chandelier holds mementos in the dining room,
where Charlotte Perriand chairs are paired with a Saarinen table, and a sunburst mirror
by Mike Diaz toes a sumptuous line between primitive and refined.

How has the South shaped your aesthetic?

There is a collective history and a tradition of storytelling that comes with living in the South, and I think this plays a strong role in my work. I've always been a modernist at heart, which influenced the architecture of my own house, but beyond the simplicity of its form, it is a richly layered home. The interior is filled with pieces I've collected over the years, artwork given to me or created by friends, and furnishings and objects brought back from places I've traveled to. The materials, patterns, and palette are inspired by my favorite locations from around the world. It's a home that tells the story of my family and my loves and inspirations.

How does living in the South enhance your work?

The South is one of the most culturally dynamic regions in the country, and it breeds a creativity that's in our DNA. Living in Charleston transformed the way I think about decorating. I was always attracted to modern design, but living in a city so steeped in history required me to think differently about how I create a space.

What's a Southern rule you refuse to follow?

I'm sure I break a lot of them. I've never been traditional in my tastes, and I've always bucked the system in some way. When I was first starting out as a decorator in Charleston almost 20 years ago, the city was changing quickly, and I felt it, but traditional decorating was still the mainstay. I was being asked to repurpose family heirlooms, which allowed me to expand my point of view and continues to strengthen the quality of my work. I built my decorating business on a juxtaposition of old and new. Breathing a modern sensibility into this centuries-old Southern town catapulted my career.

What are some of your favorite details in your house?

I am filled with joy every time I enter my house. The pivoting front door was inspired by one in a private home by Luis Barragán that I toured while on a trip to Mexico City. And although the house is small, it was important that I have a proper foyer. The floor is a blue Moroccan zellige tile in a classic Seville star pattern, with a large yellow globe light—vintage from Paris—hanging above. I feel like the sun is rising and setting over the ocean each day. Some of my favorite pieces live in the foyer: A large Uchiwa floor lamp by Ingo Mauer, a painting by Spanish artist Gloria García Lorca, and a clay mermaid sculpture by a Mexican artist that I acquired from my friend Ruth Runberg upon her return from Oaxaca. I'm also an avid reader and I love to collect books. I was a graphic designer before I became an interior designer, so unique and beautifully designed volumes are like art for me. I keep many of my favorites in the cypress bookshelves that fill one end of my living room. On the opposite side is my kitchen, which I wrapped in another zellige tile from France. I love the nontraditional pattern and the warm palette of yellow and terra-cotta. It's one of the most beautiful and textural moments in the entire space.

Hranowsky's foyer reads like a thesis statement for her passions, mixing materials, eras, and colors: a work by Gloria García Lorca, a pendant light that Hranowsky likens to a sunrise, bright turquoise tile floors, and an iconic Uchiwa floor lamp by Ingo Maurer.

Working with architect Johnny Tucker, Hranowsky plotted a structure
that would reinterpret standard Southern touchstones—like a wraparound porch
and an indoor-outdoor vibe—in a thoroughly modern way.
OPPOSITE: The cantilevered overhang keeps sightlines unobstructed.

The sofa, in a Jim Thompson print, enlivens an otherwise neutral palette in the living room and reflects the subtropical climate outside the windows. The bookcase frames art by Ramon Garcia (top) and Don ZanFagna.

Hranowsky purchased the vintage floor lamp by Carl Auböck before the foundation of the house was even poured, knowing that she'd find a place for it. The stools were found in Mexico City. OPPOSITE: The kitchen's sunny backsplash is made of zellige mosaics; the curtains feature a hand-painted motif Hranowsky commissioned from artist Beth Williams.

CW Stockwell's classic Martinique wallpaper was reinterpreted in a painterly
palette (inspired by David Hockney) by Voutsa. A lacquered
mirror reflects a Frida Kahlo cameo by Doug Meyer. OPPOSITE: Prado linens
by Matouk Schumacher dress the bed.

Lee Ledbetter

Architect and Interior Designer

"I was born in Monroe, Louisiana, and studied at the University of Virginia and at Princeton, then worked in Chicago and New York before moving back to the South in 1993 to be closer to family. I bought a midcentury modern house with my husband, Douglas Meffert. Noted New Orleans architect Nathaniel 'Buster' Curtis designed and built the house for his family in 1963, and it was listed on the National Register of Historic Places in 2014. The house beautifully marries interior and exterior spaces with full-height glass walls that become the thinnest membrane between interior rooms and their corresponding enclosed, landscaped courtyards."

The large courtyard, with vintage sets of outdoor furniture by Billy Haines and
Maurizio Tempestini, blurs the line between indoor and outdoor living.
The early 20th-century Kiks.ádi totem pole was purchased in 1965 by the house's original owner,
architect Nathaniel "Buster" Curtis, in Juneau, Alaska.

What defines Southern living for you?
Two things jump out: The confluence between inside and outside and the love for sharing your home with friends. We are very intentional in my practice about designing interior and exterior spaces in tandem, creating a "conversation" between the two. This notion is not new, but the Southern climate, with its short, comfortable winters and long summers, seems to beg for this.

Tell us about a few things that make this house so special.
I love that it's a "secret" house whose interior and exterior spaces exist entirely behind a wall. The house also occupies a large lot on a dead-end block with no through traffic, contributing to the quiet and sense of solitude. The architect, Curtis, prioritized the bouncing of natural light around the interior spaces. The floors are highly polished white terrazzo, many of the walls are partial height, and the millwork throughout is raised nine inches off the floor to allow natural light to travel over walls and below cabinets and room dividers.

How do your surroundings foster creativity?
New Orleans is one of the most unique American cities, with its melting pot of cultures—Native American, French, African, Spanish, and English—that have influenced the city's food, music, architecture, language, and customs. But it is not said often enough that New Orleans could exist *only* in the South—it is an inherently Southern city. The rich African influence would not exist here were it not for the painful legacy of slavery and the contributions of both enslaved and free people of color. The proliferation of courtyards and gardens wouldn't exist without the influence of the Spanish and the subtropical climate of the coastal South. The culture of entertaining owes its roots, to some degree, to the French settlers and planters who would return to the city after each harvest to celebrate. The cultural mix has led to tremendous invention.

Why do you think Southern hospitality is so legendary?
I was taught by example to take an interest in people, so much so that it became habit. Both of my parents came from families who entertained—my mom's is from New Orleans and my dad's is from Birmingham—and they were raised to always ask a lot of questions. I think that type of interest in others morphs into forming friendships and wanting to share your home.

What role does quirk or character play in Southern houses?
"Quirk" or "character" are what make a house a home. I've been criticized for incorporating period French chairs and antique carpets into modern interiors and architecture, but I appreciate how antiques come loaded with familial meaning and stories; they also speak to the history of my city and the homes of my ancestors. Finally, they add a layer of richness to what might otherwise be a predictable interior.

What do people get wrong about the South?
I think there's a misconception that Southerners are traditional, and yet I find that modern regional art and design have long flourished here. So many Southerners love beautiful homes and gardens, and I think the value assigned to good design gets extended to many periods of design.

The house, entirely hidden from the street with a wall, unfolds in a series of intimate spaces like the piano courtyard, bound by steel frame windows that gently delineate sightlines and help organize living spaces.

In the living room, genre-spanning furnishings—Louis XVI–style armchairs with seating by T. H. Robsjohn-Gibbings and Harvey Probber and an antique Oushak rug—are grounded by whitewashed brick walls and cool terrazzo floors. A mixed-media work by Robert Helmer (left), Jim Bird painting (far right), and Pamela Sunday sculpture (on the cocktail table) mingle with glazed ceramic vessels.

The house was originally constructed with nine-inch gaps between the floor and bottom edge of kitchen cabinetry to allow light to bounce through to interior spaces.
OPPOSITE: The breakfast room has space enough for dining around a Noguchi table and lingering on a Pierre Jeanneret chair.

Napoleon III chairs in the formal dining room are upholstered in turquoise velvet, with vividly mismatched lemon-yellow backs. OPPOSITE: To highlight original petal terrazzo tiles in the dining room courtyard, Ledbetter removed ground cover and replaced it with gray river stones.

Amelia Handegan

Interior Designer

"**I**n 2010, my husband, John Roven, and I bought this 1940s beach shack that was a 15-minute drive from our main residence in downtown Charleston. We wanted a place on the ocean that our family could visit and where we could all enjoy the outdoors. In the beginning, we decided the house should be very undone, plain-Jane, with no frills. We added onto the original structure to have more space for guests and then began updating the interior finishes. We opened the ceilings up to the rafters and installed paneling on the walls—there's not an inch of exposed Sheetrock in the house. I used raw cypress in some places and white-painted planks everywhere else. They are purposely imperfect, and I asked the installers to leave a dime's-width gap between the boards. Flash forward 10 years and the pandemic hits. We closed up our place in town and moved to Folly Beach full-time. We're on a peaceful part of the island, and if you walk a mile south, you reach a county park, where you can watch the sun set. We were hooked. We never went back downtown."

An 18th-century Italian portrait, part of a pair that Handegan found at the Round Top Antiques Fair, looms over a 19th-century Jamaican mahogany bar cabinet and adds a depth of color to the white space.

What defines Southern living to you and how does that play out in your house?

Layers, history, a sense of occasion. I don't think of myself as a traditionalist, but I do think of myself as a preservationist and restorer. I love old houses. That sense of dimension is what I missed the most when we moved to Folly full-time. So I started to bring in bits and pieces that I had in storage—antiques and textiles and especially art—to make the house feel more like every other place I've lived in, just without the grand rooms. Sometimes I still just want a "real" living or dining room, but we do have the outdoors. What I did find out is that I didn't necessarily need an 18th- or 19th-century house to accommodate all the things I love. Without a doubt, proportion and simplicity with character is an incredible backdrop that complements both humble and special pieces.

How important is a sense of character in Southern houses?

Character is everything. It's about people having things they really like around them. It's not so planned. I just buy things I love without knowing where I'm going to put them. Like the pair of 18th-century Italian portraits in my dining area: It's a couple, a man—I call him the captain—and his wife. Everyone comes in and says,

"Why do you have them there?" But I think they're hysterical! They just kind of fit and bring a depth of color to the space. I majored in fine arts but wasn't ever a really good painter, so interiors became my canvas. As long as you have a thread, it's going to look evolved. The biggest compliment someone can give me is that a room doesn't look decorated.

Tell us about a Southern tradition you embrace.

Collecting, definitely. I can't help myself—I keep bringing things in. My desk, in front of an antique Chinese screen in my office, has no fewer than six containers on it, full of paintbrushes and pencils. The living room alone was decades in the making. The cobra sconces I bought on a trip to India 12 or 13 years ago. The Robert Kime fabric on the pillow I've just loved forever and always wanted to use. The Tuareg mat I bought in Morocco. Most of the paintings are contemporary, like the portrait by Chuck Bowdish of the girl in pink with the boots, which I've had for 20 years. They're all in original gilt frames, which elevates the Tuareg mat. The space feels easy to me, and immensely comforting, like having old friends around, because everything I bought is connected to a memory. And trust me, I have plenty more in storage.

The gallery wall in the living room embodies Handegan's passion for collecting, displaying contemporary portraits by Chuck Bowdish (center) and Heidi Becker (center, right) and an 18th-century painting of a girl (top left) juxtaposed against a custom sectional in a simple cotton canvas.

A 19th-century Virginian four-poster bed and Jamaican mahogany library table achieve a West Indian island feel in the primary bedroom. OPPOSITE: In the living room, a tree-trunk lamp gains sophistication from a pleated silk shade; slipcovers on Travis & Company armchairs follow suit with more pleats on their bottom edges.

In a corner of Handegan's bedroom, a mosaic-covered table she found in Paris 20 years ago holds a 19th-century Italian curio cabinet filled with beach finds and topped with an African coil basket.

In a guest bath, a 19th-century Asian console and vintage Turkish bowl create a vanity with a character-building sense of history. OPPOSITE: Vintage lamps on an antique Asian console give a blend of Indian textiles—diaphanous sheers on the canopies and graphic quilts on the bed—instant cohesion without capitulating into matchy-matchy expectations.

A breezy walkway to the beach beneath a raised addition features unfinished wood meant to weather and lighten with age. OPPOSITE: The outdoor shower, with shutter doors painted in Benjamin Moore's Cadet Blue, is framed by four olive trees whose fruit Handegan's husband harvests and brines.

Hunt Slonem

Artist

"I divide my time between New York, Louisiana, Massachusetts, and Pennsylvania. I rescue great houses of the Gilded Age, a period of much grander intention than today. All of them have historical significance. The Southern ones, including this one, Lakeside, are antebellum. They filmed *Beautiful Creatures*, a movie with Emma Thompson, at this house. I was born in Maine but went to Vanderbilt and Tulane and have been in Louisiana since 1972. I've been greatly influenced by my time in Louisiana from day one. I started going to Neal Auction and was just fascinated by antique furniture and the level of hospitability, the magnificent way people entertained, and I've tried to capture a little bit of that in my world down here. It's not often you can entertain in a ballroom."

The iron railings on Lakeside, built in 1832, were imported from France. Its facade has been pink for as long as anyone in the small Louisiana community can remember.

Asian porcelain, a 19th-century marble, and a Parian bust mingle with Slonem's own iconic rabbit paintings in the sitting room. OPPOSITE: In the dining room, the expansive table is set with Paris porcelain. The silver candelabra and crystal chandelier both date to the 19th century.

The first-floor entryway gleams with an Empire sofa in a glinting—and historically appropriate—silk, set beneath a kaleidoscopic array of Slonem's own paintings.

Tell us your favorite things about living in the South.
Louisiana is one of the happiest places; there's a sense of festivity and celebration. I wake up in a panic in New York City, but I wake up happy here. I love the food and the music and the French influence. I love the great gardens and plants—the live oaks of Louisiana are so much a part of what makes it so different from anywhere else. Seeing all the flora and fauna—the wonderful butterflies and Spanish moss dangling from the camellias—reawakens the primordial part of life that we are so distant from in city living. Architecturally, we are in a time warp of sorts, with high ceilings and great columns. I have columns all through Lakeside and big double parlors. It's bigger than life here.

How has the South shaped your aesthetic?
It has given me a great love of patina. These houses have hundreds of years' worth of histories. It's not a brand-new thing. And there's a sense of gentility, a different level of behavior. Very few people in America really have a sense of who they are and where they come from. People in the South have a healthy love of life and a sense of family and belonging. The South is full of characters, and when they embrace you, they really take you into the family. I think it's just

a way that people interact—there's an enthusiasm for people and life, an emphasis on dance and music, an appreciation of the arts in general that's very widespread. And so many great writers have come out of this mix.

Tell us what makes your house so special.
All of my houses thrill me to the ends of the earth. They are all very grand and full of history. Each one has a grand presence and character that's formed by at least 150 years of interesting living. They are filled with stories, stories galore.

How do you entertain?
Having access to great food helps, and a spectacular setting in which to do it. I like having people over because they just melt into the house. Everyone's fascinated by the environment. I love meeting new people and listening to people tell stories and the stories about who they are—it's like a puzzle how everything and everybody fits together.

Tell us five things every Southern house should have.
A tester or half-tester bed. Lots of pier mirrors. Plenty of cast-iron urns. Camellia trees. Spanish moss. And 16-to-20-foot ceilings.

The blazing shade of turquoise in the sitting room (Giverny Green by Ellen Kennon) is a vivid backdrop for 19th-century Japanese woodblock prints and art by Slonem.

The second floor's grand hallway offers a peek into the orange
sitting room. OPPOSITE: A collection of photographs in 19th-century frames hangs
in a bathroom atop walls cloaked in cerulean blue.

In the first-floor hallway, a sideboard holds girandoles dripping with crystal and a pair of 19th-century Louisiana portraits.

A 19th-century plaster copy of a classical sculpture augments a humble
Louisiana corner cabinet, works by Slonem, and a print of a marble relief. OPPOSITE: An antique
French crystal chandelier sparkles in a third-floor bedroom.

Rebecca Vizard

Artist and Designer

"**M**y house is a New Orleans–style farmhouse-slash-lake-house-slash-hunting lodge. When I told our architect, Michael Carbine, that was what I wanted, he laughed and said, 'Good luck,' but that's what he gave us! I live here with my husband, Michael, our Brittany spaniel, Lucille, and our rescue beagle, LouLou. I'm a born-and-bred Southerner. I tried to escape when I was in my early 20s but failed miserably. It was the best failure I ever had. I love where I live and who I live with."

Vizard, who collects antique fabrics she repurposes for pillows and other accessories, groups embroidered embellishments salvaged from ecclesiastical garments with a 19th-century priest's stole in her studio.

The brick-paved breezeway, painted in a custom shade Vizard mixed on-site, connects the main house to the studio. The ivy climbing up the ceiling was a mistake that Vizard decided she liked—so much so that she even kept it when the gardener misunderstood instructions and cut the vine at the base so it died.

How does your house embody Southern living?
The easy flow from inside to out. I love the sound of screen doors swinging; it was part of the soundtrack of my childhood (that and ice clinking in my parents' cocktail glasses)—even our dogs have little screen doggie doors, and they are always running in and out. I love the way our house is nestled in nature between giant live oaks and beautiful Lake Bruin. And every room has a window to this world. When you are upstairs, you feel like you are living in a tree house. On the ground floor, you're right on the lake. Friends will pull up in their boats and, if we're not on the dock, they honk till we come out.

How has the South shaped your point of view?
I didn't realize this until my book publisher, Suzy Slesin, walked into my house and said she could tell I was inspired by my environment. I had never thought about it, but the colors in the great room are red and grungy green, like the trunks of the crepe myrtle trees outside. The other colors—grays, blues, greens, and whites—are the colors of the lake, the trees, and the sky. I was floored because I'd always thought my inspiration came from my travels, but Suzy nailed it. We also have a lot of objects from nature that we see as pieces of art, like a dead trunk from a cypress tree that makes a beautiful sculpture in the corner of the red room.

How do your surroundings make you more creative?
I definitely believe that more access to nature because of the better weather helps stimulate creativity. Growing up in the very rural South, we always had to make up our own fun, which took a lot of imagination. There were no malls or places to go hang out. We spent a lot of time outdoors and a lot of time making things out of found objects. I am grateful that my children grew up in a similar world. My son made a huge fort in front of our house that was a cross between something out of *Robinson Crusoe* and a landfill. We dubbed it Fort Eyesore. It kept him busy for years, much to our aesthetic dismay.

Tell us about some of your favorite pieces.
One would be our big pine sideboard in the kitchen that came from a restaurant in France. It stores a ton, has a lot of soul, and has seen many good times. And I love the walk-through armoire (yes!) that goes from our bedroom to the bathroom. Once, when I was visiting a friend in Paris, she pointed to a big deep armoire when I asked for the restroom. I was very confused but opened the door and discovered a powder room. (The sink was in the side of the armoire!) This gave me the idea to use one in our house and install shelves on the sides to hold towels. Every time I walk through it, I feel magical. It must be where I get my superpowers.

ABOVE, FROM TOP: The house fronts Lake Bruin and affords easy access to the outdoors from a variety of vantage points, including a screened porch. Birdie, Vizard's granddog, runs down the dock. OPPOSITE: The entryway is flanked by topiary that Vizard sculpts herself.

For the living room walls, Vizard topped a custom color with ocher glaze; the chandelier was made with corks by a community group that Vizard mentors. The armchairs hold B. Viz pillows in melon velvet and raised gold embroidery with an Ottoman Empire provenance.

In the breakfast room, Louis XVI-style chairs are matched to an unusually large antique wine tasting table. Vizard and her husband collect shed antlers (set atop the 18th-century French *vaisselier*) on walks in the woods. OPPOSITE: Built-in cupboards embrace the bed in a guest room where a vintage Kyrgyz Suzani covers the headboard beneath a gilt herald that Vizard found in an antique shop.

In the primary bedroom, an antique armoire was retrofitted as a passageway to the bathroom.
Vizard found the crystal chandelier at Scott Antique Markets in Atlanta.
OPPOSITE: A Gustavian clock secretary commands the landing at the top of the stairs; the hand-painted
Greek key fabric on the curtains was designed by Vizard for Coleman Taylor Textiles.

Nancy Braithwaite

Interior Designer

"I grew up in Chicago. My husband, Jim (also a Northerner), and I moved to Atlanta decades ago when a job opportunity for him enticed us. We raised our two daughters, Kiery and Chaffee, here; they are now grown and live with their own families in Atlanta. I live in a historic New England–style farmhouse designed by the renowned Atlanta architect James 'Jimmy' Means— just right for this transplanted 'damn Yankee.' Alongside architects Philip T. Schutze and J. Neel Reed, Means was instrumental in shaping the city's architectural landscape, and especially its houses."

American 19th-century baskets line the sill of a window that looks onto the garden designed by landscape architect William Smith, with cement-and-bronze sheep by François-Xavier Lalanne.

In the living room, an American sawbuck table holds a graduated set of antique burl wood bowls beneath a 19th-century hand-painted chandelier, displaying Braithwaite's penchant—and genius—for repetition and scale.

How has living in the South shaped who you are?

The friendships I've made, especially those with artists and craftspeople, have profoundly enriched both my life and my career. Deanne Levison, the expert on American antiques, introduced me to an entirely new world of quality and authenticity. She taught me how to see in a completely different and informed way, educating me about the Southern country antiques that we began collecting and that are intrinsic to the design of our home today. There's the work I've done with Jill Biskin, the fantastically talented painter, that gives our house in Atlanta and so many other projects I've designed so much character. The same is true about meeting Mary Jackson, the basket maker who's renowned for her expressiveness in this traditional craft. Being introduced to her work had a monumental impact on me. We commissioned her to weave a basket for our house in Kiawah. I said, "Let's do a great big one." It's probably one of the most important baskets—and the largest—that she has ever woven, and now hangs in the Gibbes Museum in Charleston.

What makes Southern homes so singular?

When I started collecting with Deanne, she suggested that Jim and I tour historic houses in the South. There's a real lifestyle involved in these houses. Newly built ones can be very special, but I'm not sure if they have the soul—the old soul—that the historic homes in the South have. When people walk into those homes, they feel their history, they sense the ghosts, and they recognize that sense of soul immediately.

What should every Southern house have?

Every house, Southern or not, needs to be a livable house. For me, this means that nothing is too precious to use. Everything within the walls of the house—and outside, too—has to become a part of your everyday activities and express your likes and dislikes. When that happens, it creates an atmosphere that's totally unique to you and your family.

Why is character so important in a home?

For people who are passionate about their homes, no matter where they are, character and livability matter. I want our home to be livable and comfortable, to have all the old-timey attributes that drive good design and that endure—a table within reach to put down a drink, a light so you can read. But if I had to choose, I would say the quirkiest thing about our house is probably the way I've placed things, which is not what most people would expect. I love to knock people's socks off with the power of scale. I love playing the game of big, bigger, biggest, and small, smaller, smallest. They're different, but equally impactful. The first grabs right away, while the other offers a slow burn of interest as it draws the eye ever closer. Repetition helps amp up the visual power. The two combined—scale in the sweet repeat—are unbeatable.

Antique barnwood ceilings and French limestone floors bracket the distilled-to-its-essence sunroom, where a totemic 19th-century gilt eagle stands sentry above the mantel. OPPOSITE: In the dining room, nail head trim has the effect of millwork and delineates a 19th-century Shaker cupboard.

Antique chairs with their original cowhide seats hang in a hallway with walls
delicately embellished by painter Jill Biskin. OPPOSITE: A striped
antique rug doubles as a tablecloth in the dining room, setting off a collection
of ceramic jugs and a Japanese maple topiary.

Hand-painted polka dots envelop a guest bedroom, where every other element in the space—
from the antique linen bed hangings to the 19th-century tête-à-tête in its dark
original finish—is perfectly attuned to walls' starring role. OPPOSITE: The graphic pattern
is based on 18th-century American motifs.

"Quirky houses create wonderfully quirky people— and all my favorite people are rife with quirks."

– Mimi McMakin

ACKNOWLEDGMENTS

*I would like to extend heartfelt thanks to the following people,
without whom this book would not have been possible:*

The creative professionals featured on these pages, who generously gave of their time and energy in answering my questions and sharing their homes. Your stories made this book come alive.

My mentor, Dara Caponigro—your taste, knowledge, and expertise are a fountain of inspiration. Thank you for your unwavering vision, strength, and commitment to beauty. It's an honor to be a part of your team.

Timur Yumusaklar, one of the most brilliant humans I've ever met. Your pioneering spirit and courage to evolve never cease to amaze me. Thank you for supporting me in my many endeavors over the years and for your unrivaled and fearless leadership.

Mario López-Cordero, my very first "work" friend and one of my dearest "real" friends. Your advice, honesty, and humor are precious gifts. Thank you for being my copilot on this journey and for cultivating and finessing the important stories in this book.

Stephanie Diaz—you do so much, so tirelessly and efficiently, and you do it so very well. Thank you for shepherding me through this process. We are all so lucky with you leading the charge!

Emma Bazilian, thank you for your many gifts—writing, editing, and an enduring love for all things classic and traditional! Your support and encouragement are invaluable.

Aaron Garza, thank you for your imagination and talent. Watching how you made every house blossom in these pages was nothing short of breathtaking.

Isabel Molster, your fortitude and hard work are what made this book happen. Wise beyond your years, you give me faith in the next generation of editors and design-lovers. If they are half as smart, industrious, and gracious as you, we are in good shape.

Kate Gilhool and Ellee Dukes, thank you for patience, understanding, humor, and hard work. I love working alongside you. Watching your creativity flourish is thrilling.

The design community—thank you for being a tight band of brilliant visionaries and a wellspring of innovation that makes the world more beautiful.

The talented photographers whose expertise brings every house, room, and sofa in this book to life. We could not tell these stories without your ability to capture the essence of a home.

The entire FS&CO family for fostering a workplace filled with boundless creativity, and the Schumacher Board of Directors for their leadership and guidance.

The Schumacher, Pozier, and Puschel families, for weathering all the storms so that we might shine bright today. Thank you for protecting this company and everything it stands for.

Elizabeth Mayhew, thank you for giving me my first job in publishing. You were singularly instrumental in shaping my sense of style—scallops, ruffles, and Arabesques are forever part of my design DNA. (And your nickname for me, "Elly May," was a harbinger of this book!)

My boisterous family—Mom, John, Faith, Matthew, Adam, Alyssa, Bob, Rocio, Brittani, Luke, Mimi, Calvin, Ben, Uncle David, Jesse, Hillary, Cody, Mary, Mabel, Uncle Mark, Aunt Gretchen, Max, Mollie, and Liz—thank you for your deep love and support. I can't wait to celebrate with you!

My beloved girls, Franny and Lucy: You give me a reason to do better and be better. One day we'll have our very own house, I promise. I love you both more than you'll ever know.

God, thank you for your everlasting love and for blessing me with an insatiable, unquenchable curiosity!

PHOTOGRAPHY

Melanie Acevedo (PP. 4, 98, 101–109, 220–227)

Cedric Angeles (PP. 13–19)

Mali Azima (P. 55)

Anna Routh Barzin, courtesy of Artsuite (P. 77)

Fernando Bengoechea (P. 8)

Sara Essex Bradley (P. 264)

Nick Burchell (PP. 2, 124–133)

Paul Costello (PP. 4, 7, 8, 74–76, 78–79, 81–85, 110–123, 154–165, 241–249, 298–309)

Peter Frank Edwards (PP. 199–207)

Pieter Estersohn (PP. 263, 265–271)

Emily Followill (P. 100)

Laurey Glenn (PP. 89–91, 95)

Vendome Press / Jessica Glynn (PP. 144–146, 148–153)

Austen Hart for Dyad (P. 42)

Stephen Kent Johnson / OTTO (PP. 135–143)

Max Kim-Bee (PP. 4, 8, 62–73, 272–283)

Julia Lynn (PP. 250–261)

Nick Mele (P. 147)

John Neitzel (PP. 284–288, 290–297)

C. W. Newell (P. 23)

Kathryn Wray Rogers (PP. 40, 43–49)

Lisa Romerein (PP. 58–59)

Annie Schlechter (PP. 87–88, 92–94, 96–97, 166–175)

Brandon Schulman (P. 289)

Warner Tidwell (P. 179)

Simon Upton / The Interior Archive (PP. 51–54, 56–57, 61, 228–239, 311–318)

Peter Vitale (PP. 8, 20–22, 24–29)

William Waldron (PP. 4, 188–197, 208–219)

Simon Watson (PP. 176–178, 180–187)

Paul Whicheloe (PP. 31–39)

Brie Williams (P. 80)

First published in the United States in 2024 by Schumacher Books
Frederic Media
459 Broadway
New York, NY 10013

Distributed by Monacelli
A Phaidon Company
111 Broadway
New York, NY 10006

Southern Interiors: A Celebration of Personal Style
By Tori Mellott with Mario López-Cordero
Copyright © 2024 Schumacher Books
Photography copyright © artists

Author: Tori Mellott with Mario López-Cordero
Graphic Designer: Aaron Garza
Art Director: Stephanie Diaz
Editor: Emma Bazilian
Editorial Director: Dara Caponigro
Publisher: Frederic Media

Printed in China
ISBN: 978-1-58093-674-3
Library of Congress Control Number: 2024937206

Visit us online:
schumacher.com
instagram.com/schumacher1889
youtube.com/schumacher1889
pinterest.com/schumacher1889